M000044887

THE VALUE
of
RADICAL THEORY

**An Anarchist Introduction to
Marx's Critique of Political
Economy**

by Wayne Price

THE VALUE
of
RADICAL THEORY

**An Anarchist Introduction to
Marx's Critique of Political
Economy**

by Wayne Price

AK PRESS

EDINBURGH · OAKLAND · BALTIMORE

The Value of Radical Theory: An Anarchist Introduction to Marx's Critique of Political Economy
© 2013 Wayne Price. This edition © 2013 AK Press (Oakland, Edinburgh, Baltimore)

ISBN: 978-1-939202-01-7 | eBook ISBN: 978-1-939202-02-4
Library of Congress Control Number: 2012955526

AK Press   AK Press
674-A 23rd Street   PO Box 12766
Oakland, CA 94612   Edinburgh EH8 9YE
USA   Scotland
www.akpress.org   www.akuk.com
akpress@akpress.org   ak@akedin.demon.co.uk

The above addresses would be delighted to provide you with the latest AK Press distribution catalog, which features the several thousand books, pamphlets, zines, audio and video products, and stylish apparel published and/or distributed by AK Press. Alternatively, visit our websites for the complete catalog, latest news, and secure ordering.

Visit us at:
www.akpress.org
www.akuk.com
www.revolutionbythebook.akpress.org

Printed in the United States on acid-free, recycled paper.

This is an expanded and revised version of material that originally appeared at www.anarkismo.net. Special thanks to Charles Weigl for his editorial work in helping me to express myself as clearly and directly as possible. All errors, of course, are mine.—WP

"The transcripts of the 2006 meetings [of the governors of the Federal Reserve Board and the presidents of the 19 regional banks, two years before the Great Recession]...clearly show some of the nation's pre-eminent economic minds did not fully understand the basic mechanics of the economy that they were charged with shepherding. The problem was not a lack of information; it was a lack of comprehension, born in part of their deep confidence in economic forecasting models that turned out to be broken."
NY Times **January 13, 2012**

"Just as the *economists* are the scientific representatives of the bourgeois class, so the *socialists* and the *communists* are the theoreticians of the proletarian class."
Karl Marx

CONTENTS

Introduction

THE world is facing major upheavals—political, military, ecological, cultural, and even spiritual. Clearly this includes a deep economic crisis, one that overlaps with all others. We need to understand the nature of the economic crisis if we are to deal with it.

When it comes to theories about the economy, the two main schools are both bourgeois, in the sense that they advocate capitalism. Both the conservative, unrestricted-free-market school (in its monetarist and "Austrian" versions) and the liberal/social democratic Keynesian school exist to justify capitalism and to advise the government on how to manage the capitalist economy.

The only developed, alternate economic theory has been Karl Marx's. His theory was a detailed and well thought-out guide for the working class, to help it understand the capitalist system in order to end it. Other radicals, particularly anarchists, developed certain topics relating to economics, such as the possible nature of a post-capitalist economy. But no one developed an overall analysis of how capitalism worked as an economic system as thoroughly as Marx. Therefore I will be focusing on Marx's work, even though I am an anarchist and not a Marxist (nor an economist for that matter). I do not accept the total worldview developed by Karl Marx and Friedrich Engels, even though I think much of their analysis is accurate.

When people write about "radical economics" they generally mean two interrelated topics. One is an analysis of the currently-existing capitalist economy. The other is the vision of a post-capitalist, post-revolutionary, economy. From these two topics, it is possible to develop a strategy for getting from one to the other. When it comes to an analysis of capitalist economy, Marx's economic theories are superior to others, including what there is of anarchist economic thinking. In *An Anarchist FAQ*, Iain McKay writes that there are "subjects anarchists have, traditionally, been weak on, such as economics" (2008, 13). Anarchists have certainly made contributions, but there is no coherent "anarchist economics" in this sense. While Proudhon may have come closest, neither he nor other anarchists developed his insights into a full system comparable to Marx's work. However, when it comes to presenting a post-capitalist vision, a socialist goal, then anarchism (with other, non-Marxist, libertarian socialisms), I believe, is superior to Marxism. This is not to deny that Marx made useful contributions, but nothing he or Engels suggested is as clear or coherent as the anarchist program. Taken together, the two theories are greater than the sum of their parts.

I make no claims for originality. When there are differing interpretations of Marx's theory, I may take a minority position, but I remain focused mainly on Marx's concepts, as expressed in the three main volumes of *Capital*, the *Grundrisse*, and a few other works, and in the work of his close collaborator and comrade, Friedrich Engels. I will not engage the Marxist theories of post-Marx commentators, many of whom disagree with fundamentals of Marx's views—rejecting, for example, his labor theory of value and his analysis of the tendency for the rate of profit to fall. Many reject the idea that state capitalism is possible. In fact, most are *de facto* advocates of state capitalism, in the sense that most social democratic/reformist Marxists call on the existing state to intervene in the economy, in order to bolster capitalism, while most revolutionary Marxists seek to replace the existing state with a new state, replacing the bourgeoisie with state ownership—while maintaining the capital/labor relationship.

There are many introductions to Marxist economics, starting with Marx's own *Value, Price, and Profit* and his *Wage-Labor and Capital*, and including vast numbers of more sophisticated works on the topic. Very rarely, though, has an anarchist written one for anarchists and other libertarian socialists. I suspect it may be useful today.

Can Anarchists Learn from Marx?

Some anarchists have been offended by my even raising the possibility that they might benefit from studying Marx's work. They point out, correctly, that the First International was torn apart in a bitter factional fight between the followers of Marx and those of Michael Bakunin, the founder of anarchism as a movement. The Second (Socialist) International did not even let anarchists join. Following the Russian Revolution, the regime of Lenin and Trotsky had anarchists arrested and shot. In the Spanish revolution of the 1930s, the Stalinists betrayed and murdered the anarchists. Marxism, as an organized political tradition has led, on the one hand, to social-democratic reformism and support for Western imperialism. In other cases, it has evolved into a form of mass-murdering, totalitarian, state capitalism (misnamed "Communism") before, in countries like China and the Soviet Union, collapsing back into traditional capitalism.

There is no denying any of that—and no need to deny it. I am not debating the merits of Marxism or anarchism as social movements or historical traditions. Nor am I interested in trading tit-for-tat accusations about whether Marx or Bakunin had the more authoritarian personality, or whether Proudhon or Marx first came up with this or that economic idea. I am an anarchist, which should tell you which social vision I ultimately find more compelling. But that doesn't mean I cannot see the importance of Marx's critique of political economy. My goal is to help anarchist readers do the same. Even at an introductory and generalized level, Marx's theory presents a fairly accurate model of contemporary capitalism and its future. I hope revolutionary anarchists find this helpful.

Both Marxism and anarchism grew out of the nineteenth century socialist and working class movements. Both had the same goals of the end of capitalism, of classes, of the state, of war, and of all other oppressions. Both focused on the working class as the agent of revolutionary change, in alliance with other oppressed parts of the population.

Yet anarchists rejected Marx's concepts of the transitional state ("the dictatorship of the proletariat") and a nationalized and centralized post-capitalist economy.

They rejected his general tendency toward teleological determinism and his specific strategy of building electoral parties. Instead, anarchists sought to replace the state with non-state federations of workers' councils and community assemblies, to replace the military and police with a democratically-organized armed people (a militia) for as long as necessary, and to replace capitalism with federations of self-managed workplaces, industries, and communes, democratically planned from the bottom up.

None of this has prevented many anarchists from expressing appreciation for Marx's economic theory (see Schmidt & van der Walt 2009, 85). Historically, as McKay points out, "Both Bakunin and [Benjamin] Tucker accepted Marx's analysis and critique of capitalism as well as his labor theory of value" (2008, 24). Carlo Cafiero published his own summary of *Capital* in 1879. More recently, Cindy Milstein, an influential US anarchist, wrote in *Anarchism and its Aspirations*, "More than anyone, Karl Marx grasped the essential character of what would become a hegemonic social structure—articulated most compellingly in his *Capital*" (2010, 21).

To some extent, these anarchists believed that it was possible to divorce Marx's economic theory from Marx's political strategy. Some radicals argued that there were two sides to Marx's political and economic insights—and I agree (see Aronson 1995; Sherover-Marcuse 1986). Marx could, at times, espouse visions that were libertarian, democratic, humanistic, and proletarian, while, at other moments, recommend more authoritarian, statist, and bureaucratic strategies. He could be alternately scientific and open minded, or determinist and scientistic.

Stalinist totalitarians managed to employ both sides of Marx's Marxism. They most obviously used the centralizing, authoritarian aspects, but Marx's positive, libertarian and humanistic aspects also played a role: the ideological one of painting an attractive face over their monstrous reality. They have misled hundreds of millions of workers and peasants in mass movements that thought they were fighting for a better world. Does that mean that libertarian socialists should reject all of Marx's work, even the positive aspects? What would happen if we did? When it comes to economics, if we abandon Marx's system, we are essentially left with bourgeois economic theory, rationalizations of a social system that also has a history of bloodshed, mass suffering, tyranny (including racial oppression and Nazi genocide), and two world wars. This is not a superior record.

There has long been a minority trend within Marxism that has based itself on the humanistic and libertarian-democratic aspects of Marx's concepts. This goes back to William Morris, who worked with Engels in Britain while being a friend of Peter Kropotkin. It continues with today's "autonomist" Marxists (who sometimes call themselves "left communists"). The version of Marxist economics I learned was heavily influenced by the "Johnson-Forrest Tendency" (the pseudonyms of C.L.R. James and Raya Dunayevskaya) and by Paul Mattick of the "council communists." My point is not that these libertarian Marxists had the "true" understanding of Marxism, as opposed to the authoritarianism of Marxist-Leninists. I am simply saying that, empirically, it has been possible for some to combine Marxist economic theory with a politics that was very close to anarchism. My own anarchism has also been enriched by feminism, classical liberalism, radical psychoanalysis, progressive education, Malcolm X's thinking, ecology, and non-anarchist decentralism, among other influences—as well as by aspects of Marxism. Openness to different trends of thought is something which I find valuable in anarchism.

I therefore have two goals here. Besides explaining Marx's economic theory and letting people make up their own minds about it, I hope to show anarchists that it is possible to learn from aspects of Marxist theory while remaining anarchists. We do not have to reject everything written and done by Marx and Marxists in order to be anarchists. We can learn from, and possibly surpass, Marxist theory.

Marx and Proudhon

Anarchists often raise another complaint about Marx's political economy: that he did not invent his theory by himself but learned it mostly from other thinkers, including Pierre-Joseph Proudhon, the first person to call himself an "anarchist." They denounce Marx as a plagiarist.

There is no question that Marx made a thorough study of thinkers who went before him, including bourgeois political economists and socialist writers. His writings, published and unpublished, often read like dialogues between himself and earlier economists (e.g., his *Theories of Surplus*

Value, the "fourth volume" of *Capital*). This is another part of what he meant by his "critique of political economy." He claimed to go beyond them but he never denied that he built on earlier thinkers. Some political economists he respected (particularly those in the line from Adam Smith to David Ricardo). Others he despised (the pure apologists whom he called "vulgar economists" or "prizefighters").

When Marx and Engels first read Proudhon, and then Marx met him in France, they were impressed. Coming from the background of a working artisan, Proudhon had developed a critique of capitalism and a concept of social-ism. The two young, middle-class, radicals learned from him. In *The Holy Family* (the first really "Marxist" book), Marx and Engels commented on Proudhon's 1840 *What is Property?*: "Proudhon subjects private property, which is the basis of political economy, to a critical examination…. That is the great scientific progress that he has achieved, a progress which revolutionizes political economy and which present, for the first time, the possibility of making political economy a true science…. Proudhon does not only write in the interest of the proletarians, he is a prole-tarian himself" (quoted in Jackson 1962, 47).

Later on, Marx and Engels became political and theo-retical opponents of Proudhon. Marx attacked his views in *The Poverty of Philosophy*, as did Engels in *The Housing Question*. Bakunin stated, "There is a good deal of truth in the merciless critique [Marx] directed against Proudhon" (quoted in Leier 2006, 230). I am not going to get into the theoretical questions that were debated; that is a task for another book. I believe that Marx and Engels learned much from Proudhon and then developed past him in certain ways. Beside immediate economic theory, Proudhon developed a program that was an early version of "market socialism" to which democratic communism was superior. More positively, Proudhon worked out aspects of decentralized-federalist socialism, which was contrary to Marx's centralist statism. Some of Proudhon's concepts were important in the later development of revolutionary anarchism. In brief, there were things that Marx and Engels learned from Proudhon; things that they developed further; and things that they might have learned from him but did not.

In any case, the key question should be whether or not Marx's economic theory is a good theory, useful for understanding the capitalist economy, and useful for developing political reactions to it. If he got good ideas from Proudhon or anyone else, then good for him.

Critique of Political Economy?

What sort of theory was Marxism, exactly? There is some dispute over whether one should refer to "Marx's economics," "Marx's political economy," or "Marx's critique of political economy." As to the first, Marx discussed the production and distribution of commodities and other typical subjects covered by texts on "economics." At the same time, his goals and interests were entirely different from those of bourgeois economists. He was not an economist. He was not interested in explaining "how capitalism works" for the sake of objective, disinterested, science, nor was he advising capitalists how to manage their economy.

Marx wanted to explain capitalism to the workers and their allies, to help them to become conscious of their situation and to aid them in changing it through revolution.

As for "political economy," this is a term taken from Aristotle, who distinguished between "domestic economy" (of the household and the farm) and "political economy" (of the polis, the overall community). Early bourgeois economists picked up the term. They integrated their analysis of economics with a wider understanding of the role of classes and the state. Modern radicals often adopt the term in order to emphasize that they are doing the same, embedding economics within the social totality.

Marx himself, however, generally used "political economy" as a synonym for bourgeois economics, and the phrase, "critique of political economy" to describe what he was doing. It was the title or subtitle of several of his books (including *Capital*). The term "critique" meant "a critical analysis," examining the positive and negative aspects of something, in their interactions. He was an enemy of the political economists, however much he respected a few of them for their insights. He was the opponent of the system he was examining—and exposing. Some Marxists today prefer to say they are furthering the "critique of political economy." Yet it does seem a lengthy, somewhat awkward and archaic phrase. Almost no one refers to "critiques" today outside of literary discussions.

I use all three terms for Marx's economic theory, but it is essential to keep in mind that we are developing an attack on bourgeois economic theory and the capitalist economy. In a very real sense, the whole of Marx's *Capital* was a justification for what he wrote as the conclusion of the *Communist Manifesto*, "The proletarians have nothing to lose but their chains. They have a world to win. Workers of all countries unite!" as well as the first "rule" of the First International, "The emancipation of the working classes must be conquered by the working classes themselves."

The Value of Radical Theory

Why is radical theory, anarchist and Marxist, so important, so valuable? Because the socialist revolution is different from the bourgeois revolution. In the bourgeois revolution, what was essential was the sweeping away of all the barriers to the free development of the capitalist market: the aristocracy, the bureaucratic state, the privileges of the guilds, and so on. Then the "invisible hand" of the competitive marketplace would work (more-or-less) on its own, automatically developing industry and trade. The middle class revolutionaries did not have to fully understand what they were doing, so long as they cleared away the barriers to capital accumulation. The rebellious artisans and peasants were not allowed to understand that they were overthrowing one ruling class (the aristocracy) only in order to replace it with another (the bourgeoisie).

But in the socialist-anarchist revolution, the working class and its allies among the oppressed can and must understand all that they can, as clearly as possible. They have no automatic market to organize for them; on the contrary they have to organize to replace the market. They have little previous experience in actually managing organizations, compared to what the bourgeoisie had before their revolution; they have to gain organizing experience in the course of the struggle. They are dealing with an interconnected industrial and economic social machine, which requires cooperation on a vast scale; therefore it needs the fullest democratic participation of everyone, at every level, and in every way.

All this requires collective, democratic decision making, class consciousness, and as much theoretical understanding as is possible, on as wide a basis as can develop. Therefore there is value in radical theory, including an anarchist understanding of Marx's critique of political economy.

Part I:

Basics

Chapter 1:
The Labor Theory of Value

Marx's Method

BEFORE looking at Marx's theory, I should say something about his method. I will start with his belief that what we empirically perceive with our senses is just the surface of reality. The sun appears to go from east to west in the sky, over a flat earth, and we rightly guide ourselves by this when we travel for most distances—even though we also know that the earth is round and goes around the sun. When I touch the top of a table, it feels hard and solid, and in one sense, it is: It resists the pressure of my hand. But it is also true that the table is mostly empty space composed of whirling subatomic particles.

The same is true for society. There is surface and there is depth beneath that surface. Both are valid views of reality, different perspectives on reality, equally true (in the sense of being useful in their appropriate context).

How do we find out, scientifically, what is behind the obvious surface? We cannot bring the economy into a laboratory, nor can we do controlled experiments (not ethically, anyway). Marx's method is *abstraction*. Mentally, he abstracts (takes out) aspects of the whole gestalt, while temporarily ignoring other aspects of complex reality. The very field of economics is an abstraction, because it separates (in our minds) processes of production and consumption from other social processes, such as art and culture, politics and religion.

Using abstractions, Marx built theoretical models of the economy. For example, in order to understand commodities, he imagined a society based on simple commodity production, a society of small, independent farmers, small shop keepers, merchants, and artisans, buying and selling goods and services (commodities) from each other. It was not a model of a capitalist economy, because these hypothetical workers owned land and shops. No one was forced to work for a wage nor to submit to capitalist bosses. Such a society has never existed. Isolated pockets have, at the margins and in the cracks of larger (slave or feudal) societies, but Marx postulated it as an entire society in order to begin his examination of commodity production and exchange.

Marx next imagined an economy with an industrial capitalist class and the modern working class, but with no landlords, no peasants, no merchant capitalists, no bankers, no middle classes, etc. Creating such a model (of an imaginary capitalism), he explored how it might work. He wound the model up and watched how it ran. Gradually, he added more and more aspects of the actual society to his models—such as other classes (merchants, bankers, landlords, peasants, etc.)—hoping to gain insight into how the whole, complex, messy, real society works.

Abstraction has permitted Marx's critique of economics to remain relevant through a century and a half of further development. Despite changes, capitalism still survives and its basic structure is still in operation. Marx was looking for the underlying, recurring, patterns of mass behavior known as economic "laws." But these laws never appear in pure form in any actual society. Their effects are interfered with, mediated, and countered by other forces. They show up in the long run, cumulatively, and in modified form. Therefore Marx repeatedly said that economic "laws" are more properly seen as "tendencies." To see how they really work out, we must move beyond abstraction and analyze each situation in its concreteness.

Three Factors?

According to Marx, when we concretely analyze most societies, at least since the rise of class society, we see that economic systems historically have been based on various forms of inequality and oppression. Ours is no different and the imbalances start right at the foundations.

For bourgeois economists, production in every economic system requires three "factors" or "inputs": land (not just soil but all natural resources), labor (people), and capital (here meaning tools, machines, buildings, etc.). Each factor must be paid for and, under capitalism, this means rent for land, wages for labor, and interest for capital ("interest" here being a euphemism for profit). Since, the economists tell us, all three factors contribute to production and all are paid for, there is supposedly no exploitation. Yet, if this three-factor model applies to all societies, it must apply to feudalism, to classical slavery, and to every past exploitative society. These were societies where ordinary people had to work longer and harder than they would have to survive, because most of their labor went toward supporting the ruling minorities.

Marx claimed that this was also true for the modern working class, the "proletariat" (a term from ancient Rome that meant "those who do nothing but breed"). While capitalism looks, on the surface, like a society based on equality, Marx sought to demonstrate (as we shall see) that it was as exploitative a system as slavery—that the capitalist class (or "bourgeoisie") also lived off the surplus labor of the workers. However, even without a full Marxist critique, it should be obvious that the payment for each factor of production is not equivalent. Wages are paid to workers for doing work. Rent is paid to land owners for letting others use their land. Interest (profit) is paid to the capitalists for letting others use their capital. While land and machines are clearly necessary for the workers to produce goods, landowners and capitalists—the *people* who own land and capital—do not actually contribute anything.

Alienation and Fetishism

The concept of alienation (estrangement) was fundamental to Marx. In his view, what makes people human is our capacity to produce, to create what we need out of the environment, using our physical and mental labor. Under capitalism workers are forced to labor, not for themselves but for someone else. Indeed, since profit may flow toward distant, possibly unknown people and institutions, to corporations or government agencies, workers labor for *something* else: the system of capital itself. The harder they work, the stronger and larger becomes capital, which rules over them, drains them of their energy, and increases its power, due to their efforts. This is alienated labor. All the institutions of society are alien powers ruling over the working class.

Under such conditions, people develop unhealthy forms of "projective identification," (a term from psychoanalytic object relations theory). People feel empty, hollow, and weak. They feel powerless, despite the fact they are the ones who *make* the world. They project their actual inner strength onto some symbol or institution: the flag, the leader, a nation, a football team, or their version of God. By identifying with such things, they can access the strength they believe they have lost and feel whole again, for a while.

When identification meets the realm of political economy, it becomes what Marx called "fetishism." Early people worshiped idols and special objects (fetishes), regarding them as having their own powers and personalities. People in advanced bourgeois society also treat objects as if they were alive and powerful. On a theoretical level, economists describe "land" and "capital" like living beings that confront "labor." In our everyday lives, we are surrounded by commodities with human qualities—sexy cars, friendly software, revolutionary dish soap, intelligent microwaves. Marx compares this to the mysticism of religion. Commodities seem to exchange and circulate themselves independent of us. Like an empty, foreclosed house to the family evicted from it, an assembly line to the worker sweating away at it, or a gold necklace to the person wearing it, objects and machines seem more real and vibrant, more important and in control, than human beings. Marx's critique, however, sees through this alienation to the reality that it is people who are interacting with each other, through their use of machines and objects, and not the other way around. Under capitalism, human social relations begin to appear as external "things" that "happen to" us, when they are actually relationships among people, interactions between workers and capitalists.

The Nature of Value

Commodities—objects produced for sale—have two aspects. Each commodity is a specific object, a baseball, say, or a hammer. It has a use and it was made in a specific way with specific machines through a specific labor process. But each commodity is also worth a certain amount of money. A number can be attached to it, denoting its monetary value: $1, $10, or $1 million. Every commodity is money-fiable. In Marxist terms, these two aspects of a commodity are known as "use-value" and "value" (or—combining the two—"exchange-value").

The capitalist management of a business does not really care much what the use-value of a commodity is. They are not necessarily going to play with the baseballs or build with the hammers they produce. Their only concern as capitalists is that someone else finds the baseball or hammer useful and, therefore, is willing to buy it. Capitalists only want money. They produce baseballs and hammers in order to end up with more money than they started out with when they hired workers and bought machinery and raw materials. They seek to expand the total value they have to accumulate ever more value, not to increase society's share of useful goods. As Marx writes of the capitalists' main drive, "Accumulate, accumulate! That is Moses and the prophets!... Accumulation for accumulation's sake, production for production's sake" (1906, 652). This is why capitalists are willing to kill the last whales. When the whales are gone, the capitalists will simply take their profits and invest in something else, such as cutting down redwoods. The commodities (and the raw materials they require) are more or less interchangeable; the important thing is the profit they generate.

The question of how the value (and, therefore, price) of a commodity is determined is absolutely central to Marx's economic theory. The process of answering it helps reveal the inner workings of capitalist society. So, what is this thing called "value," this thing that all commodities have, which makes them able to have a monetary value (price)? *There is something which is not money in itself, but that can be expressed in money.* Some claim that it is based directly on generalized utility (use-value). However, air is the most useful stuff around, and it has no price. In an attempt to get around this problem, post-Marxist economists have developed the theory of "marginal utility," which tries to combine use-value with a measurement of how much or how little a consumer already has of a commodity (satiety and scarcity) and, thus, how strong the demand for it might be.

Scarcity and satiety can make a difference in the short run. In 1996, there was a sudden mass desire for a particular Christmas gift: the Tickle Me Elmo doll. The manufacturers had not made enough for the market, so the price shot up. But over time, seeing that there were not enough dolls for everyone who wanted them, the manufacturers expanded production until they had matched demand (or went beyond it). This is the tendency of capitalist production: to match supply to demand, overcoming scarcity.

Of course, there are some things that remain scarce, no matter how much money is offered. There will be no more Rembrandts (although market pressure does inspire forgers). Paintings are not a major part of the economy, but other things may be. I will discuss monopoly later (both natural—as in the Rembrandts—and artificial—as in diamonds which are deliberately kept rare and therefore artificially costly).

However, even leaving aside the tendency for supply and demand to balance themselves, the theory of marginal utility has another major drawback: The use-value of any object (aside from something like air) is very subjective, enough so that it makes a very poor indicator of anything. Even regarding food and drink, which we all must have, people vary enormously in their tastes. How then does a society develop a unified set of prices for all objects?

For Marx, what commodities have in common is labor. People work to produce them and, in a sense, commodities can be seen as condensed versions of the work that went into them. This, in an admittedly simplified form, is what is known as the "labor theory of value," and it's really the only way of calculating value and price (or beginning to do so) that makes sense. In a nutshell, it means that commodities exchange at equal values due to equal amounts of labor-time put into making them.

Marx himself never made an elaborate argument for his labor theory of value. He did not have to. Almost every political economist he read already used some version of a labor theory of value (including Smith, Ricardo, and Proudhon). It was common sense, especially because, unlike our semi-automated present, the ratio of human labor to machines was heavily weighted toward labor. It seemed intuitively obvious that labor created wealth. In fact, the bourgeoisie used theories of the centrality of human labor in producing value to attack their class enemies, the landlord-aristocracy, as unnecessary parasites.

Once the capitalists became the ruling class, Marx, Proudhon, and others used the labor theory of value to attack *them* as unnecessary parasites. At the same time, the ratio of machinery to labor expanded hugely, helping to obscure labor's role. This allowed professional (bourgeois) economists to abandon the labor theory of value. At first, as we have seen, they tried "marginal utility." When that proved inadequate, they mostly gave up having any sort of value theory at all. They stuck to the surface level of prices and ignored the issue of underlying value. Practical businesspeople had never been very interested in value theories anyway.

From Value to Price (Part 1): Labor, Living and Dead

Value is the foundation of monetary price and labor is the foundation of value. For this introduction, I am using "value" and "exchange value" interchangeably (although Marx made a distinction between "value" as the pure labor-time, and "exchange value" as value with a use-value). Only human beings can add value to a commodity through labor. While it might seem as if a robot or baseball-making machine does pretty much the same thing as a worker making balls by hand, the machine doesn't create value. The machine *has* value and can *pass on* increments of its value, but that's all. Let's say that a capitalist buys a baseball-making machine for his factory and that the machine, over the course of its life, can manufacture a million baseballs. With each baseball it makes, the machine "uses up" a portion of its value—what we call "depreciation" (the machine wears out bit by bit as it is used). That depreciated value is passed onto the baseball (in our oversimplified example, the value would be one-millionth of the value of the machine). A machine can only transfer portions of the value it already has (in theory, the capitalists add the cost of the depreciation onto the price of each baseball, save the results as a depreciation fund, and eventually use the fund to buy a new machine when the old one has worn out). And where did the baseball-making machine's value come from in the first place? From the labor of the men and women who made the machine. No matter how automated a production process appears, if you "follow the value," you'll always find human labor at the end of the line, extracting raw materials, transporting and transforming them, not to mention continuously maintaining, repairing, and operating the machines.

When capitalists invest in what is necessary to produce commodities, what they buy can be lumped into two categories. First are the raw materials that will be worked up into the final product, along with the tools and machines that will be used. Then there is the labor power of the workers hired to make the product.

The first category (materials and machinery) is known as "constant capital," because its value, however it is passed on, remains constant. The value of the leather or other covering is entirely passed along to the baseball. The same is true of the fuel that is used up in running the machines. Machines and tools don't pass on their total value, since, as we've seen, they are not used up in making each baseball (the capitalists will add a cost to the price of the balls to create a fund for buying new machines when the old ones are worn out). The completely used-up raw materials and fuel are called "circulating constant capital." The machines and tools are "fixed constant capital."

But the second category, the labor of workers, is different. Labor changes things. It adds value that did not exist before and lays the basis for profitable production. Therefore it is "variable capital." Add constant and variable capital together and you get the "cost of production," a necessary factor in determining a commodity's price.

However, when determining the value of a commodity (the basis of its price), we need to step back and look at the big picture. What matters is not how much labor actually went into making a specific object, but how much *socially necessary labor* went into it. Labor is mostly measured in time: the time it takes to make something. A factory with obsolete machinery will take more labor time to make a commodity than a plant with up-to-date machinery. One might expect that the commodities made the old-fashioned way, with more labor, would have higher prices. But customers usually will only buy commodities at the cheaper price (the ones made more efficiently). Therefore, if the capitalists with the old machines want people to buy their goods, they will have to sell at the new, lower price too. So, in general, most of the commodities will sell according to the *average* socially necessary labor incorporated into the *average* product on the market. The extra labor expended by using the old methods of production will be wasted. Similarly, if more of a specific commodity are produced by all the capitalists than there is a demand for in the market, then the labor that went into producing the extra commodities has been wasted. This lowers the value of the commodities (and lowers the prices, due to lesser demand).

While commodities made with new methods, using less labor, tend to be cheaper this can sometimes be hidden by other factors. For instance, the (temporary) monopoly held by more advanced producers might let them jack up their prices. But this will eventually be offset as other producers get the same new machinery.

The labor that goes into a product has a dual aspect. One is the "concrete labor" of a specific worker making a specific object, with its specific uses (its use value). The other is better seen as "abstract labor." It is a fraction of the total labor used in the whole society, an abstraction that, in turn, allows labor to be translated into an exchange value (expressed in money) that corresponds with all the other exchange values. There is a tendency for all labor to be turned into abstract labor by modern capitalist industry, as it de-skills individual jobs. The trend of capitalism is for every commodity to be made, not by one craftsperson at a bench, but by the labor of a large number of people, in a sense by the whole society. It is impossible to really say exactly how much each individual worker adds to a product that has gone through a whole factory, beginning with the raw materials worked up by masses of other workers. Each commodity really represents a fraction of the total labor of the collective workers of society. What really matters to the capitalists is their firm's total wage bill and the total amount of time it takes to make their products.

The Most Peculiar Commodity

Before going further in understanding the relation of value and price, let us look at the unusual commodity that is at the heart of capitalist production: "labor power." Labor power is the ability of the worker to work, and it is a commodity because the worker must sell it to a capitalist. Labor itself, the actual swinging of hammers or washing of dishes, is not a commodity, because it is a process. The commodity that capitalists buy is the workers' *ability* to work, to use their hands and muscles, their brains and nerves, in the service of capital. They buy the *capacity* to work, not the work itself. Labor power is an unusual commodity. It is attached, so to speak, to human beings with minds and consciousness, which they must subordinate to the production process. It alone expends human labor, which is the only way of creating new value.

How do we determine the value of this unusual commodity? Following the law of value, its worth (expressed monetarily in wages or salaries) is based on the amount of socially necessary labor that goes into producing it, what it costs to "reproduce" workers every day so that they are able to show up at work. Classical political economists expected capitalism to drive down workers' wages to a biological minimum, whatever rock-bottom standard is necessary to just keep workers alive and able to breed a new generation of workers.

Of course, as Marx pointed out, there are also cultural, historical, and "moral," factors that capitalists must take into consideration. On the one hand, modern industry requires a level of education and culture that was unnecessary when capitalism began. On the other, working people in each society are used to a certain level of food, clothing, shelter, medical care, culture, and entertainment—a standard of living. This is based on their country's history, which includes past struggles to prevent themselves from being driven down to a biological minimum. The value of labor-power as a commodity is not something that is just imposed on the workers by the capitalists but is the result of an interaction, a two-sided struggle.

Some workers are much more skilled than others, usually workers who have had years of training. This includes skilled blue-collar workers, but also many white-collar "professionals" (teachers, engineers, etc.) who, like other workers, labor collectively for bosses who give them orders. Marx says that the economy treats the value of their labor power as worth several times that of the general value of unskilled labor power, due to their training. The fact that their labor is worth more adds more value to the product. In practice though, the collective labor process and the total labor market smooths out these differences in wages and salaries; what is significant to the owners of each capitalist enterprise is their total wage bill. This is a major part of their total costs and, therefore, of the eventual price they will charge for their commodities (and therefore for each commodity). As I will discuss later, the functioning of a capitalist society depends on its total production of value (including "surplus value") in all its enterprises, and this depends on the collective labor of all its workers—whatever their levels of skill.

Capitalists usually regard the workers' standard of living as "too high" (that is, too costly in wages and in taxes for public services). The capitalists would like to lower the working class's standard of living, to redefine the value of the commodity labor power and thus increase their own profits. But the bosses must be careful not to attack workers too directly, which might provoke resistance. But when the economy hits a crisis, the capitalist class may feel it is necessary to attack the living conditions of the working class, that is, to lower labor power's value—if they can.

An intensified attack on the value of the workers' labor power has been going on in the United States and other industrialized countries for several decades now. As we have seen more and more lately, when it cannot be done through peaceful, "democratic," means, the capitalists may eventually turn to state repression in order to attack the workers' standard of living. And, if the workers resist, this will deepen the economic and political crisis.

Freedom and Equality under Capitalism

Unlike previous toilers, modern workers are "free" in some ways. Certainly, they are not owned by a master or lord; they are not slaves. Unfortunately, many other aspects of capitalist "freedom" are a bit more dubious.

On the surface, in the labor market, workers meet capitalists as apparent equals. Capitalists sell their commodities (goods and services) to the workers, who buy them with money. Similarly, workers sell their commodity (labor power) to the capitalists, who pay them money. Superficially, profits are not gained through exploitation, but by an apparently equal exchange. This formal equality corresponds with the formal equality of bourgeois democracy, where each citizen gets one vote in elections, regardless of race, religion, country of origin, or gender. Dig a little deeper, however, and things get more complicated. Discussing capitalist "freedom," Anatole France wrote in 1894, "the law, in its majestic equality, forbids the rich as well as the poor to sleep under bridges, to beg in the streets, and to steal bread."

Workers are also "free" in the sense that they don't own the machines, factories, offices, tools, raw materials, and land needed to do their jobs (the "means of production"). They are "free" to sell their labor power to the capitalists who do own all those things, but if they refuse to do so, they and their families are "free" to starve, or at least to be driven to the wretched bottom of society. Capitalists control a crucial part of the production process and, under capitalism, workers must play by their rules in order to live. They have the freedom to choose which boss will exploit them—and sometimes not even that.

Once workers enter the workplace, even their formal equality is gone. Now the capitalists (or their managers) are in charge, giving orders, and the workers become subordinate, following orders. Whether or not workers can vote in government elections every few years, once inside the workplace—for most of their waking lives—they live under despotism. They can be fired at any time for almost any reason. Only the few who belong to unions have some limited rights—and it's important to remember that unions only exist because workers fought for them, not as a result of any bourgeois interest in equality.

Once again, Marx's critique of political economy looks behind the surface of equality and democracy to the reality of capitalist despotism—and to the reality of the workers' daily struggle against that despotism.

From Value to Price (Part 2): Surplus Value and Profit

Returning to the relation of price to underlying value: My next step is to discuss the nature of profit and where it comes from.

It is common to see profit as resulting from the process of selling or "circulation." Each capitalist tries to buy needed materials cheap and to sell finished commodities dear—at as high a rate as the market will bear. So profits seem to come from selling commodities above their values. This may be true in a limited sense, for individual firms, but it cannot explain how it works on a societal level for the whole capitalist class. That is because, for each capitalist who sells a product at a price above its value, there is someone else (a consumer or another capitalist) who is losing money by paying extra for it. This includes the same capitalist who buys needed materials to make this product in the first place. *Everyone* cannot sell commodities at a higher-than-justified level. The result would be inflation of overall prices, but not the creation of profit. All of which suggests we must look for the origins of profit in the field of production, not circulation.

When bourgeois economists, and even many non-Marxist radical economists, try to explain profit in terms of production, they offer a seemingly obvious answer: profits come from the expansion of production. The idea here is that combining land, labor, and capital produces more commodities than previously existed. That "more" is the profit. Once again, though, this theory does not hold up very well.

Suppose the workers in a factory produce a hundred baseballs in five hours, but then new machinery lets them produce two hundred baseballs in the same amount of time. Does this create a profit of one hundred extra baseballs (a 100 percent rate of profit)? Not really. It does create more use-values, because there are more baseballs for people to use. But the capitalist owners are not interested in creating more useful things for people. They want more exchange value (in the form of money). If twice the number of baseballs are now produced in the same time, each baseball will be cheaper than before, perhaps 50 percent cheaper. Ignoring the costs of the raw material, one hundred baseballs used to be worth five hours of labor, now two hundred baseballs are worth five hours of labor. There are more things and more utility but not more exchange value. Without an increase in exchange value, there is no increase in total value and therefore no profit (how "extra baseballs" does increase profits in a roundabout way will be discussed).

For Marx, profit, like monetary price, is based on labor time. Workers toil for an agreed-upon amount of time, let's say eight hours a day, at an agreed-upon wage, let's say ten dollars an hour, or eighty dollars a day. At a certain point during their work day, they will have produced commodities with enough value to pay for their wages. They have produced (after, say, two hours) eighty dollars worth of baseballs, a figure equal to the value of their labor power for the day—the amount needed for their families' food, clothing, shelter, education, and cultural needs. That two hours was the "necessary labor." But they do not stop working after two hours. They continue to work, with a break for lunch, for a total of eight hours. Those final six hours are unpaid. They are "surplus labor." They are work done for free, just as slaves or serfs did free work for their lords. The extra labor produces extra value, described as "surplus value."

From this surplus value, created by the unpaid labor of the workers, comes the profits of the investors in an industrial enterprise, the profits of retail merchants, the loan interest collected by banks, the rent to landowners, advertising fees, taxes paid to the government, etc. This surplus value from all the capitalist enterprises supplies the income of the entire capitalist class, and its hangers-on. The capitalists use it for buying luxuries, but mostly for reinvesting in industry—to expand constant and variable capital for the next cycle of production, which will create more surplus value, and more profit. This is the accumulation of capital.

There are two basic ways capitalists can increase the amount of surplus value they pump out of the workers. One way, called "absolute surplus value," is to increase the length of the working day. Since "necessary labor" (what is necessary to pay for the value of the commodity labor power) stays the same, the amount of surplus value will increase. This method was used mostly in the beginning of industrial capitalism. Workers, including child laborers, worked twelve or fourteen, or more, hours a day. One problem with this approach is that it tended to physically weaken the working class, because they were, in effect, being paid less than the biological minimum. This, of course, threatened to undermine the whole system. Nonetheless, this method is still used, in factories in Asia and elsewhere, and even in the United States, through compulsory over-time in many industries.

The other method produces "relative surplus value." Without lowering the amount the workers are paid, capitalists decrease the amount of time workers spend producing their wage-equivalent (the necessary labor). This can be done by speeding up the assembly line, by time-and-motion studies (Taylorism), by increased productivity through better machinery, or in other ways.

There are limits to both methods. The main one is that the day is limited; even Superman cannot work more than twenty-four hours in a day. Lesser mortals reach their biological limits, from lengthened days or from speed-up, well before that. These limits push the working class to fight to defend its needs, to resist its exploitation, even as it has to accept the basic social relations of capitalism.

And what does this have to do with price? The price we pay for a baseball, like the value of any commodity, is equal to the cost of constant capital (whose value was created by past labor and is now passed on incrementally to the finished product) plus variable capital (new value created by labor and paid for) plus surplus value (new value created by labor but not paid for). This is true for the individual commodity and for the mass of commodities, for one baseball or thousands.

From Value to Price (Part 3): Price of Production

However, this creates a conceptual problem. The ratio of exploitation is the ratio of surplus value to variable capital (unpaid labor to paid labor). Capitalists definitely care about this; they want to get as much labor out of the workers as possible. But what they are *most* concerned with is the ratio of surplus value to their total investment, which is constant capital plus variable capital (i.e. the cost of production). They do not care, nor are they even aware, that only living labor (variable capital) can create surplus value. They are only looking at their bottom line.

Imagine two factories with the same number of workers (living labor) working the same hours at the same rate of pay. They have the same rate of exploitation, of surplus value to variable capital. The two factories will produce the same amount of surplus value. Will the capitalist owners receive the same profits? Not necessarily. Suppose the two factories produce two different commodities, requiring different machinery and raw materials. Therefore each has a different amount of constant capital (dead labor). Perhaps, one has a lot, one has a little. Here "profit" is surplus value as a proportion of the total cost of production. The capitalist with the large amount of constant capital will have a lower total profit than the one with the lesser amount of constant capital, even though the rate of exploitation is the same in each factory.

However, in reality, industrial capitalists do not get smaller profits because they buy more efficient, productive machinery, which permits them to hire fewer workers. If they did, capitalists would not innovate by investing in better equipment. There would be no accumulation. The rate of profit does not seem to be (directly) controlled by the amount of labor used in production. Does this disprove the labor theory of value?

Marx solves this dilemma, once again, by stepping back to look at the big, societal, picture. Industrial production that gets high rates of profit (because of extra surplus value or any other reason) attracts other capitalists. These new capitalists invest in the profitable industry and expand production of its commodities. This competition drives down prices and therefore drives down profits. Eventually the profits are no longer especially high; they are about the level of the society's average rate of profit. The same thing, in reverse, happens in industries that have especially low rates of profit (due to large amounts of constant capital or any other reason). Capitalists will withdraw from that industry, or they will just produce less. With fewer commodities being available to the market, the price will go up and so will the rate of profit per item. Eventually its profit rate will also be approximately at the average rate of profit.

The way it works out, it is as though all the surplus value produced in society is pooled together and each capitalist producer gets to share in it, not according to their number of workers but according to their amount of invested capital. Marx calls this de facto sharing "capitalist communism." There is an average rate of profit, which is the ratio of the total surplus value of a society to the total invested capital of society.

So, we can now reconceptualize the value of a commodity as the "price of production." This includes the "cost of production" (variable capital plus constant capital) plus *an average profit*. Actual prices fluctuate due to the multiple pressures of supply and demand in the market, but they fluctuate around the price of production. Capitalists will not sell commodities for less than they cost to make, (constant + variable capital) nor below the average rate of profit (at least not for long!). And selling them above the average rate of profit only attracts others to compete by underselling through lower prices.

While focusing on production, Marx's theory does not deny the significance of subjective demand, which is central to the bourgeois economic theories. First, Marx says that capitalists will not produce commodities unless they believe that there is a market (demand) for them, that is, that the commodities have use-value for someone with money to buy them. Second, Marx says that the labor used to make more commodities than there is a demand for (in the marketplace as a whole) is wasted and does not add to the value of the commodities. Third, the surface prices are assumed to fluctuate around the price of production, the fluctuation itself being due to rises and falls in supply and demand.

One other major factor may influence prices. This is monopoly. If one firm dominates an industry, for whatever reason, or if a few firms do, they can set prices and not worry about competitors selling at lower prices (in bourgeois economic terms, they are "price makers" rather than "price takers"). They can sell above the average rate of profit, taking an extra large share of the total capitalist class's surplus value (resulting in less profit for the smaller, competitive, firms). There are limits to this also; I will discuss monopoly in a later chapter. (Land ownership is also a form of monopoly. Marx has a discussion of ground rent, which I am not going to cover in this work.)

Now I have presented a simplified version of Marx's concept of how values get to be expressed as prices and how surplus value gets to be expressed as profits. And, in the process, Marx has revealed some of the inner workings of capitalist society, how the logic of the capitalist production process has specific social and political effects, including exploitation, inequality, authoritarianism, and most importantly, class struggle.

Anti-Marxist economists focus on the relation between value and price as a central problem. They call this the "transformation problem," although Marx does not actually see labor-time values as being "transformed" into monetary prices. Rather he presents price and labor-time as two ways of expressing value. The "price of production" is how the market reorganizes commodities' labor-time values due to the pressures of competition, not the abolition of their values. As this is an introductory text, I am not going to review the attacks on Marx's value theory and the Marxist responses (see Kliman 2007). Marx was not really interested in specific prices. He held that the total of all society's values, measured by socially-necessary labor time, was equal to the total of society's prices (a concept somewhat similar to the "Gross Domestic Product"). As mentioned, he held that the total of the surplus value was equal to the total of all profits, and that this could be used to find the average rate of profit. These were his key concepts.

For Marx, *the essential, defining, concept* of capitalism is not competition, private property, nor stocks-and-bonds. *It is the capital/labor relationship.* On the one hand capital is driven (by class conflict and by competition) to expand and grow, to accumulate ever more value. He defines "capital" as "self-expanding value." If a company does not continually expand, it will eventually be beaten by its competitors and go broke; if the capitalist class as a whole does not keep expanding, it loses domination over the proletariat. Capital is represented by its agents, the bourgeoisie and their managers.

On the other hand is the proletariat, those who have nothing but their ability to work, with muscle and brain. They sell their labor-power to the agents of capital, who proceed to pump surplus value out of them by working them as hard as possible and paying them as little as possible. This is a relationship; without capitalists there are no proletarians; without such modern workers, there are no capitalists.

(To clarify a point: when Marx wrote about classes, such as the proletariat, he meant it as a whole slice of the population. That is, the proletariat as a class was not just employed wage workers, but also their dependents, such as children and women who are full-time homemakers, also retired workers, not to mention unemployed workers. Similarly, the bourgeoisie was not only those who personally own stocks, but also their families. Capitalism is a relation between classes. In a total sense, one class lives from the labor of another whole class.)

Money

Value, when expressed as price, requires the existence of money. Money is both a measure of value and a store of value. Originally, humans used only valuable things for money: cattle, or belts of shells (wampum). After a long history, they settled on gold and silver. These are rare metals found and dug up by labor. They had original use-values in that they were used for decorations. They last indefinitely, without rusting. They are easily divided into small units and easily merged back into larger ones. Small units may represent a lot of value. Governments produced official coins, backing their value with the power of the sword.

In pre-capitalist societies, money was peripheral, as were commodities in general. Most objects were made for family use or for neighbors. Only a few commodities were sold on a market. But in order to live under capitalism, we rely on acquiring commodities for everything, from everyone, throughout the world. Now money is an essential intermediary, the "universal equivalent," which holds all of society together in a "cash nexus."

As capitalism developed, it became inconvenient for merchants to lug around large quantities of metal. Banks were created to hold the gold. They provided banknotes that could be circulated and then turned in for hard money when desired. These notes were "as good as gold." Today—to simplify a long, complex history—the state issues fiat money: that is, symbolic, nominal, unbacked paper money. It is supported by nothing but the confidence people have in the health of the economy. Unlike gold (or cattle), it has only a "fictitious value," but no intrinsic value.

Chapter 2:
Cycles, Recessions, and the Falling Rate of Profit

ANY honest appraisal of capitalism must admit that it is an economic system defined by repeated cycles of crashes and recoveries, from deep downturns, through increased productivity and relative prosperity, to the next precipitous plunge. Of course, classical political economists of Marx's time, and earlier, denied the inevitability of business cycles and their crashes. The capitalist market, they held, was so efficient that it balanced what came into it and what came out, production and consumption, buying and selling, in a smoothly functioning process. There might be momentary, localized, disharmonies in one industry or another, but no overall crashes. When things went wrong, it must be due to extra-economic factors: bad weather, wars, or government intervention in the market, which, supposedly, was always a bad idea.

Yet there have been cycles for as long as capitalism has been around. These downturns were called "crashes" or "panics" until the nicer term "depression" was found. After the ten-year Great Depression of the 1930s, the milder-sounding "recession" was preferred. Today's economists do not have much of a theoretical understanding of them. But they believe that, with the use of governmental monetary manipulation, tax changes, and/or government spending, it is possible to modify the cycles, to reduce their downturns to insignificance. Too bad this has not worked out so well.

Marx was far ahead of his time in recognizing the reality of repeated business cycles and their resulting crises. He never wrote a full theory of the business cycle in a single study, but his thoughts about it are apparent, especially in his discussion of capital accumulation. However his lack of one concentrated and complete statement has led Marxists to propose various theories of cycles and their crashes.

Cycles and Crashes

One of the most widespread misunderstandings of the capitalist cycle is held by people who know only a little about Marxist economics. In its simplest form, it is known as "underconsumptionism," and its main point is that crashes happen because workers produce more than they can buy back. In other words, the consumer market cannot absorb what's been produced, capitalists cannot sell all their commodities, and this supposedly causes the system to collapse.

The problem with this view, though, is that workers *always* produce more than they can buy back, even in the "healthiest" capitalist economy. The value of the products they make is the sum of variable capital plus constant capital plus an average profit (from surplus value). Workers can only spend the sum of their wages (i.e. variable capital). They can *never* buy back the constant or surplus values. If they had to, then capitalism would not merely have downturns, it would not work at all.

Simple "underconsumptionism" is not so much a model of the business cycle but a crude intuition. A more sophisticated view is the model known as "overproduction" (or "overaccumulation"). It makes a similar argument from the perspective of production rather than consumption. Unlike the simple underconsumptionist view, this predicts periodic crises. The idea here is that, in their drive to expand, competing capitalists put more money into constant capital than into variable capital. They are constantly seeking to expand labor productivity, which means more machines and materials, and proportionally fewer workers (the number of workers may increase, but not as fast as the amount of machinery). Also, capitalists try to increase surplus value, which requires holding down workers' pay. Even in times of prosperity, when capitalists are relatively more willing to increase workers' pay, they are still reluctant to do so. As a result, production of consumer goods expands faster than the wages of the workers, production outstrips consumption. And if the consumer goods-producing capitalists (what Marx calls "Department II" of the economy) cannot sell their goods, they will no longer buy from the machinery-producing capitalists ("Department I"), who now also cannot sell their products. If goods cannot be sold, then their values cannot be "realized," and periodically things head toward a crash.

To use economist-speak, the problem highlighted by the overproduction (overaccumulation or sophisticated underconsumption) model is a lack of "effective demand" or "aggregate demand." For demand to be "effective," it is not enough that people want something, such as food: They have to have the money to buy it. ("Effective demand" is central to the analysis of liberal Keynsianism, and overproductionism leads to a rapprochement between a version of Marxism and Keynes's school of bourgeois economics.) This analysis leads to liberal proposals to try to solve downturns by raising workers' wages so they can buy more commodities and prosperity will return.

Certainly, if workers are unemployed or paid low wages, they cannot buy many consumer goods and this is bad for the capitalist economy. But the reverse, that high wages will cause prosperity, is only true in a limited sense. Workers get their wages and salaries from the capitalists who hire them. If *all* the workers spend *all* their income to buy goods sold by the capitalists, they will only be returning the money that the capitalists paid them in the first place. This will keep the wheels turning for a while, but it does not provide an extra penny of profit to the capitalist class—no matter how high the workers' wages.

Another, related, model incorporates these views, but takes them in a somewhat different direction. It is called "disproportionality." The capitalist system is a very complex system. To work, the different parts have to match up with each other. Not only must consumer goods production match the consumer market, but each commodity must match with its need. Everything has to happen to the right degree in the right order at the right time: raw materials, production of machinery, use of machinery, the right numbers of everything, the right amount of money for the different capitalists to buy the right product at each stage of production, the right workers in the right numbers with the right skills at the right wages, the right distribution of commodities, the right amount of credit, and so on. Each commodity has both a use-value and a value, so each must fit into the complex process at the right time and in the right place. All this must happen despite the fact that there is no overall plan, just a number of competing capitalist firms. While the bourgeois economists speak of the market as a smoothly running mechanism, in fact it lurches forward with herky-jerky motions. *Of course*, it produces ups and downs, prosperities and recessions.

There is much truth in each of these models of capitalist economic cycles. Certainly, if capitalists cannot sell what they produce ("realize" their surplus value), then there is a depression. But these concepts leave out what needs to be at the center of any analysis of capitalism: how profit is created in the first place (that is, how labor is exploited). This is what drives all capitalist production, what it is all about, and it makes all the difference. If the production of profit is very high, then the capitalists will expand, hiring more workers and being (relatively) more willing to increase their pay. This will expand the consumer market. Meanwhile, in order to expand, they will be more willing to buy materials and machines from each other. Higher profits prevent overaccumulation and underconsumption. Similarly, higher profits counter disproportionalities. It greases the wheels. With more profits, things go smoother and match up better. Conversely, lower profits have the opposite effect, increasing overproduction and disproportionality. There seems to be "too much" of some commodities only because there is "too little," namely too little surplus value has been produced.

The Tendency of the Rate of Profit to Fall

Each capitalist firm seeks to raise its profits by using the most modern technology, the most productive methods. This means investing in more and better machinery, in order to raise each worker's productivity. They may hire more workers as they expand, but they will buy even more machinery, and raw material to go through it. The expansion of constant capital is actually an attack on the working class, an effort to (relatively) decrease capitalists' reliance on the workers.

As a result, a company's workers will produce more goods in the same amount of time, each good cheaper than the competitor's version. The owners of the factory can flood the market with their cheaper goods—although they may charge a higher mark-up (profit) than their competitors. They will win a larger market share and make a bigger profit, which is the whole point: their greater investment gets them a larger share of the total surplus value produced by all the capitalist firms. Eventually, competitors will catch up with them by also installing new machinery. Or the competitors will go bankrupt. Either way, the original initiators will have established a new normal for productivity levels in the industry.

While this individual factory makes a larger profit, it actually contributes a smaller proportion of surplus value to society's pool than before. *Profit is nothing but the unpaid labor of the workers.* The purpose of machinery is to displace labor, to use less labor to make more things. Factory owners may have more surplus value because they hire more workers, but they have bought even more machines, so the ratio of surplus value to the total investment goes down. And when the whole industry adopts the new technology, the whole industry will be producing a lower ratio of surplus value. When most of an economy has adopted similar new technology, society's total ratio of surplus value will decrease. The total amount invested will increase, but the total amount of surplus value will not increase proportionally. The total mass of surplus value may have increased or decreased, according to the number of workers employed, but its ratio to the total invested decreases. Which is to say that the profit rate will decrease.

(To introduce a bit more Marxist terminology: The basic ratio between machinery/materials and workers is called the "technical composition." If we measure the two sides of that ratio by their values—how much each costs, in money or labor-time—this is the "value composition." Put both together and you get the "organic composition." The more machinery, the higher the organic composition—the lower the rate of profit produced.)

Classical political economists had noticed the falling rate of profit before Marx, but had no good explanation for it. In the *Grundrisse* (Marx's original notes for what became *Capital*), he said that the law (or tendency) of the rate of profit to fall "was the most important of political economy" (quoted in Mattick 1978, 191). Given the importance Marx placed on the concept, it is sometimes surprising how many Marxists, past and present, ignore or reject it. For instance, one reason the concept is so crucial is the light it sheds on unemployment in our society. The whole point of increasing machinery in production is to decrease the amount of labor used. Higher productivity forces out labor. This creates a pool of unemployed workers, a surplus population that Marx calls "the reserve army of labor."

That reserve army may increase and or decrease, but it is always there, part of the basic logic of capitalism. Some are immediately available for work (members of the "floating" reserve army of labor). Others are busy elsewhere but can be called upon if more workers are needed (referred to as the "latent" reserve army). This includes poor peasants and also women homemakers. Women may be attracted (or forced) into the labor force when there is a shortage of (mostly low-paying) labor. But most can be pressured back into the families when no longer "needed." At least that has been the history so far. And some people are simply mired in poverty and long-time unemployment: the "stagnant" reserve army. So capitalism has a long-range trend to increase the organic composition of capital, resulting in both a tendency toward a falling rate of profit and a pool of unemployed workers.

Healthy Recessions

The rate of profit affects the business cycle. As the economy expands after a downturn, the rate of profit first goes up. But once the cycle reaches its peak, the rate goes down. New machinery increases the organic composition of capital overall, which causes the rate of profit to decline. Shortages of workers temporarily increase as production expands, as do bottlenecks caused by a lack of skilled workers, and capitalists have to raise the pay of at least part of the working class. Workers are more likely to strike for better wages and conditions, and the capitalists are more willing to give in. This too lowers the rate of profit.

To keep their profits coming in, capitalists borrow money from banks and from each other. Debts pile up. They speculate, invest in shaky schemes, and buy into "bubbles." This is made easier by the split in the economy between the actual commodities, the factories, and other things that embody value because they are made by people (the productive base of the economy, which bourgeois economists call the "real economy"), and the pieces of paper that denote wealth and the ownership of those things (the "paper" or "virtual" economy). Stock certificates provide capitalists with claims on surplus value. They are bought and sold with little relationship to the actual workplaces and work processes where value is created. In Marx's terms, these are "fictitious capital." We'll discuss this in more detail in the next chapter.

Finally there is a crash. And a good thing too. The recessions are essential for the profitability of the capitalist economy. Weak companies, with old-fashioned technology, go bankrupt. Their technology is either to be junked or bought-up cheaply by better-run companies. Machinery in general becomes cheaper during the downturn. So does labor power. More people are unemployed; workers will be forced to accept lower pay. "Overproduced" goods are sold off (or destroyed). Debts and speculations are wiped out in bankruptcies. Stronger companies buy up resources from weaker ones, creating larger corporations. All these factors clear the way for a more profitable economy.

And, so, there will be a new upturn, moving toward a new period of prosperity. The collapse of the crisis was essential for clearing out the deadwood and preparing for the new and bigger upturn.

Countertendencies to the Falling Rate of Profit

There are countertendencies to the tendency of the rate of profit to fall, some of which we'll revisit in the chapters ahead. The business cycle, particularly the downturn, mobilizes these counteracting tendencies and restores profitability.

One such countertendency is the fact that the rate of turnover, from investment to the sale of products to re-investment, varies from industry to industry. In itself, this may cause disproportionality. But the more rapid the turnover, the higher the rate of profit.

Imperialism, in its various forms, also increases profits. It brings in commodities from poorer countries with lower costs (especially lower wages but also cheaper raw materials) and bigger profits than can be produced at home.

However, the main counteracting tendencies involve the very expanded productivity that (due to the increased organic composition of capital) causes the rate of profit to fall in the first place. Expanded productivity makes cheaper (less valuable) commodities. If this becomes widespread, then the constant capital bought by the industrial capitalist (the machines and materials) also becomes cheaper. If the capitalist makes the same profits as before, they are now in ratio to cheaper investment costs, therefore the rate of profit goes up.

The same is even more true for the other costs of the industrial capitalist, the workers' wages. As productivity increases in general, the goods that workers buy to maintain and reproduce themselves become cheaper. The food, clothing, healthcare, shelter, entertainment, and education that make up the cost of the commodity of labor power, all cost less labor to make (cost less value). It is now possible to lower wages and still—for a time—maintain workers' standard of living. The use-value of the goods they earn remains the same—or even increases—while the exchange value of their pay goes down. (This lowering of pay may be done by directly cutting it or—less provocative to the workers—by inflation.) So surplus value increases, without necessarily immediately lowering the standard of living of the workers.

This trend makes it possible for workers in a more industrialized country, with a higher standard of living, to be just as exploited as workers in a poorer country; that is, they may have a higher standard of living but still get the same low proportion of the values they produce. Whether this is so needs to determined by examining more than their standard of living, which can hide what is really going on.

Capitalist firms get larger and larger, more and more concentrated. This does not directly counteract the fall of the rate of profit. But it does produce larger amounts of surplus value in one place. This goes a long way toward counteracting the immediate effects of the falling rate. On the other hand, the larger enterprises get, the more capital is needed for investing in them, which a falling rate of profit makes it harder to acquire.

The tendency of the falling rate of profit is a major factor in the business cycle, behind disproportionality and overproduction. Historically, the biggest countertendency to the falling rate of profit is the inevitable downturn phase of the cycle, which restores capitalism to profitability. So the system lurches forward.

Do all these counteracting effects compensate for the falling rate of profit enough that, over the long run, it is no longer a threat? No. Over time, the organic composition of capital (including the value composition) slowly increases, despite every counteracting tendency. John Henry may have used a sledge hammer, but he was beaten by the steam drill, which has since been replaced by even more powerful equipment. Shovels have been replaced by earth-moving machines as big as houses. Steel puddling has been replaced by almost fully automated factories. Horses gave way to trucks, railroads, and airplanes. Paper and pencils to computers. True, the difference in value between a shovel and an earth-moving machine may be less than their difference in weight. Yet the tractor does cost much more. And the number of workers needed to dig the same size hole has gone way down. This creates a long-term trend toward a lower rate of profit, even though it is repeatedly counteracted by modifying factors. The trend shows itself in an eventual decline in the rate of accumulation (growth of capital) over time.

Part II:

Epochs of Capitalism

Chapter 3:
Capitalism's Dramatic Entrance: Primitive Accumulation

FOR Marx, capitalism has a beginning, a middle, and an end. Let me start at the beginning.

According to the classical political economists, when they dealt with the question at all, capitalism began with small businesses in the nooks and crannies of feudalism. These were artisans and merchants. As this story goes, these businesses gradually made more money for their owners—accumulated capital—until they could afford to hire some employees. The first workers were available to be hired because they had not been as industrious as the original businesspeople. As in Aesop's fable, the workers were lazy grasshoppers, while the original capitalists were hard-working ants. Eventually, the capitalists became rich enough to displace the feudal lords.

To begin with, this quaint story of capitalism's "natural" evolution overlooks the violent upheavals that paved the way to a new economic system: the Cromwellian British revolution, the US revolution, the French revolution, the South American and Caribbean revolutions, and the failed 1848 European revolution. Still, some of the story is no doubt true. Some blacksmiths and artisans did build up their original capital; some merchants who carried goods between widely separated markets decided to directly invest in production here and there. However, this misses early capitalism's main dynamic: war upon the working population. "In actual history, it is notorious that conquest, enslavement, robbery, murder, briefly force, play the great part" (Marx 1906, 785).

In *Capital*, Marx called this time (which I will call an "epoch" to leave room for several periods within it) a "prehistoric stage of capitalism." Borrowing from Ricardo, he described its nature as one of "primitive accumulation" (in German, *Ursprunglich*, which can just as well be translated as "primary," "original," "initial," or "unspoiled"). For capitalism to begin on a large scale, even in only one country, it needed two things: the accumulation of masses of wealth in the hands of a few people who could invest it (capital), and secondly, "free" workers available for work in factories and fields under capitalist discipline. This created the capital/labor relationship.

In Europe, these two things were achieved through violence, both legal and illegal. Starting in earnest in England in the eighteenth century—but part of a pattern reaching back to the sixteenth—a series of laws, known as "enclosure acts," drove peasants off the land by dismantling traditional land rights. Lands once held communally and open to all people for grazing livestock or mowing hay were fenced off to become the private property of wealthy landowners. This was by no means a natural process: Soldiers and private thugs burned villages and forced people to abandon their main source of livelihood. Once self-sufficient farmers were now forced to wander the roads looking for ways to survive. Additional laws were passed that ever further restricted people's options, cut benefits to the poor and unemployed, and inexorably pushed peasants toward the capitalists' factories and fields as the only way to live. Pre-capitalist forms of wealth, such as land, goods, or even people, were turned into commodities, wealth that could be bought and sold on the market.

On a world scale, primitive accumulation meant that European rulers seized entire continents and subcontinents—in the Americas, India, other parts of Asia, Australia, and Africa. Black people were forced into slavery far from their homes while Native Americans faced genocide. European people were settled on distant land once owned by others. The Asian-Indian economy was destroyed by foreign imports, even as natural resources (from gold to cotton) were robbed from them.

Marx was aware of the interaction of class, nationality, and race in the origins of capitalism. "The discovery of gold and silver in America, the extirpation, enslavement, and entombment in mines of the aboriginal population, the beginning of the conquest and looting of the East Indies, the turning of Africa into a warren for the commercial hunting of black-skins, signalized the rosy dawn of the era of capitalist production. These idyllic proceedings are the chief moments of primitive accumulation" (823).

Marxists, and even Marx himself, have criticized anarchists for supposedly underemphasizing the role of economic forces and overemphasizing the power of the state. But when discussing primitive accumulation, Marx was quite clear about the key role played by the state and other forms of organized violence. While capitalism may be said to have created the modern state, the state may also be said to have created capitalism. In *Capital*, Marx wrote of "the power of the state, the concentrated and organized force of society, to hasten, hothouse fashion, the process of transformation of the feudal mode of production into the capitalist mode.... Force is...itself an economic power" (823–824).

The anarchist Peter Kropotkin writes of the same period, "The role of the nascent state in the sixteenth and seventeenth centuries in relation to the urban centers was to destroy the independence of the cities; to pillage the rich guilds of merchants and artisans; to concentrate in its hands the... administration of the guilds.... The same tactic was applied to the villages and the peasants.... The state...set about destroying the village commune, ruining the peasants in its clutches and plundering the common lands" (1987, 41). If not precisely the same as Marx's concept of primitive accumulation, this describes the same process.

This conception of primitive accumulation might seem to contradict a class theory of the state. If the state is always an agent of one class or another, then these initial tasks of capital accumulation would require rule by capitalists. But capitalists did not exist, or at least did not dominate the state, during the late medieval-feudal period. However, both Marx and the anarchists reject a simplistic concept of history. They never claimed that capitalism and its ruling class sprang fully grown out of a suddenly dead feudalism. Rather, it slowly gathered strength over centuries. There had been a gradual expansion of markets, an increase in the use of money, the growth of a layer of merchants and wealthy businesspeople, divisions among the feudal aristocracy, and a growing state that strengthened itself by balancing among various class forces, including the nascent capitalists and the dying and/or changing aristocrats. Under these conditions, protocapitalist forces were able to use aspects of the state to forcefully help along the development of the new economic system.

Women under Capitalism

Marx did not directly discuss the effects of primitive capitalist accumulation on gender. However, his concept of primitive accumulation is directly relevant to understanding the history of women—and the role of women is essential for understanding the origins of capitalism. As with the enclosure of the commons, women were forced from their traditional roles (and traditional sources of power) into new ones within the emerging capitalist economy.

As feminist historians and specialists in religious and medieval history have shown, the sixteenth and seventeenth centuries saw a widespread persecution of "witches" in Europe and North and South America. The bloodbath, led by the church, but including state authorities, claimed that its victims were members of a heretical sect, composed almost only of women, which supposedly worshipped the devil. Special tribunals were set up, methods of torture were standardized, and witch-hunting manuals were published. The numbers of women persecuted is unknown. Some estimates run into the millions, but the best estimate is that, over three centuries, about two hundred thousand were accused of witchcraft, of whom a hundred thousand were killed (Federici 2004). It is impossible to know how many of these people were just women someone disliked, how many were midwives or herbalists, how many were practitioners of pre-Christian religions, and how many (if any) were genuine worshippers of the devil.

What we do know is that the witch hunt was a prolonged attack on half the population, mostly focused on poor women in the cities and countryside. The campaign was part of general misogynist sentiments promoted by the church and state. In a society already undergoing alarming changes, it whipped up hysteria and misdirected people's fears and angers away from the rich and toward other poor people (similar to the rise in anti-Semitism at the time). It divided working people, causing men to cling to male privileges even while their general conditions were being undermined. It drove women out of the traditional workforce, preparing them to become modern "housewives" and part of the modern working class. This was an essential part of the process of primitive accumulation.

The oppression of women, as specifically developed at the origins of capitalism, continued and continues as capitalism evolved. While Marx does not discuss the role of women in the capitalist economy, it is implicit in his theory. Female waged labor, like child labor, was common in British industry in the nineteenth century. In *Capital*, Marx describes their actual conditions in the factories and mines. He notes that they were paid less than men for the same work. That much, at least, remains the same today.

But there was another, and more fundamental role for women, which applies to them as non-waged members of the working class. The working class—*as a class*—is broader than those who are immediately employed; it includes children, the unemployed, the retired, and wives and mothers who labor in the home. The wages paid for (mostly male) workers' labor-power cover what they need to recuperate, to rest up and be able to work another day. It fell, and still mostly falls, on women as "homemakers" or "housewives" to see to it that the men regain their strength. The price of the wage (the "family wage") also covers raising children, the new generation of workers. This work also falls on the women, as does much of the task of passing on the necessary social psychology to the children through the family. In *The Origin of the Family, Private Property, and the State* (1972), Engels describes this reproductive work of women as being as much part of the "base" of society as industrial production (as distinct from the "superstructure"). He suggests that class society itself grew out of the original oppression of women.

In other words, while women at home do not *directly and immediately* create surplus value, they produce (reproduce) the necessary labor power of their husbands, children, and themselves, which is essential if surplus value is to be produced. The unwaged labor of women in the home is an essential part of the overall production of capitalist society. The oppression of women benefits men (as a collectivity), but also specifically benefits the capitalist class in its drive to maintain and expand capitalist production.

Women in upper-class families do not reproduce their families' labor power, since the bourgeoisie does not sell its labor power for production. But the haute bourgeois family is a center for maintaining and accumulating property, and wives play a key—if subordinate—role in holding the families together. Meanwhile, they help instill in the next generation the necessary social roles that allow family members to serve as the "personification of capital" in their turn.

This is not, of course, an adequate analysis of women's oppression; but it is clear that the oppression of women, in the family and in the workplace, is thoroughly intertwined with capitalist exploitation—as it had been with pre-capitalist forms of exploitation (see Vogel 1983).

African-American Oppression

Primitive accumulation also involved a vast expansion of African enslavement in the Americas. Africans were kidnapped and forcibly brought to the Americas to serve as a form of worker, namely as slaves. It was a very distorted form of capitalism, since the slaves were obviously not "free labor." But they produced commodities (tobacco and cotton) for the world market and were integrated into world capitalism. This primitive accumulation of human bodies and human labor lasted into the nineteenth century and was only ended through revolutionary violence in various countries (Haiti, the United States, parts of South America, etc.).

With the end of slavery, African-Americans served two purposes for capitalism. On the one hand, they were a pool of low-wage labor, available for super-exploited work—that is, due to their vulnerability, the value of their labor-power commodity was below that of the rest of the (white) work force. On the other hand, they were used to divide and weaken the entire working class, due to the prejudices of the white workers and their acceptances of petty privileges, at least as compared to African-Americans. This is a major reason why US workers achieved many fewer social benefits (such as universal health care) than the workers of Europe in the period after World War II. The Civil Rights and Black Liberation movement resulted in many improvements, but African Americans are still racially and economically oppressed in capitalist society, still concentrated in the working class at the bottom of capitalist society. Capitalism does not seem to be able to end its racism.

Primitive Accumulation's Destruction of the Environment

Marx and Engels understood that early capitalism was destroying the biological environment. Human labor was, for them, the way humans interact with nature, satisfying human needs while maintaining a biological balance. They saw this as a "metabolism" between humans and nature. But capitalism, they believed had developed a "rift" in the metabolism (see Foster 2000). The most important factor, to them, was the split between city and country, between industry and agriculture. This division had been noted by a number of "utopian socialists" before them, as well as by bourgeois agronomy specialists. Kropotkin and other leading anarchists (several of whom, like him, were professional geologists and geographers) were also to raise this as a problem, well before the modern Green movement.

Farms and cities were increasingly separated. Agriculture drained the soil of nutrients. They had once been returned to the soil through local consumption of food and the use of animal and human manure, but now animal and plant nutrients were shipped over increasing distances to cities. Their eventual waste was not returned to the land, but polluted cities and the rivers and lakes around them. Meanwhile, waste products from production—coal dust, dyes, cotton dust, etc., polluted the air, the water, and the food of the city's inhabitants. Engels walked through Manchester, the center of British industry, and noted the poor health of the working class, the filthy conditions they lived in, and the diseases that spread through their quarters. We have learned a great deal more since then about the ill effects that capitalist production has on the environment and on general health. But Marx and Engels saw it quite early.

During the epoch of primitive accumulation, the capitalists were able to accumulate wealth by robbing the land of its nutrients and by not paying to keep their cities clean or their working classes healthy. These were not simply matters of indifference or ignorance; they were a way to accumulate riches, to increase values.

The Epochs of Capitalism

Once it was established through violence and theft, capitalism continued, of course, to develop. In his *Grundrisse*,

Marx essentially proposed three epochs of capitalism (or two long epochs, of growth and of decline, and a brief high point between them):

> As long as capital is weak, it still itself relies on the crutches of past modes of production.... As soon as it feels strong, it throws away the crutches, and moves in accordance with its own laws. As soon as it begins to sense itself as a barrier to development, it seeks refuge in forms which, by restricting free competition, seem to make the rule of capital more perfect, but are at the same time the heralds of its dissolution and of the dissolution of the mode of production resting on it." (quoted in Daum 1990, 79)

That is, in its earliest stage, capitalism is weak. It must rely on non-market forces (primitive accumulation) to expand. It uses force, the state, religious hysteria, anti-women prejudices, robbery and slavery, and plunder of the natural environment. It brings non-European regions under the control of the protocapitalist heartland. This process began as far back as the fourteenth century, but reached its high point in the sixteenth to eighteenth centuries.

In the nineteenth century, capitalism took off, first in Britain and then as a world system. During the height of its well-being as a system, it relied mainly on market forces to batter down all obstacles to expansion (not that it abandoned imperial armed force). This was the apogee of capitalism, if a relatively short one (Amin 2012). It was also the time when working class and socialist movements began to grow. It was when Marx wrote his books and was influential in the First International—in which Bakunin started the anarchist movement—and when the Paris Commune broke out.

After this heyday comes the final epoch, capitalism's long decline, beginning in the early twentieth century, when capitalism has reached its limits and its contradictions threaten to tear apart all society. I will discuss this in the next chapter.

Marxist theorists have measured, interpreted, and subdivided capitalism's epochs in varying ways. However they do so, there generally are no sharp divisions among the epochs. They are just abstractions to help us conceptualize the history of capitalism. They overlap in their traits and tendencies. Primitive (nonmarket) accumulation, including violence by the state, continued during the height of market capitalism and has expanded again during the final epoch of capitalist decline.

Chapter 4: The Epoch of Capitalist Decline and Social Revolution

IN his preface to his *Critique of Political Economy*, Marx wrote, "At a certain stage of their development, the material productive forces of society come into conflict with the existing relations of production, or—what is but a legal expression of the same thing—with the property relations within which they have been at work hitherto. From forms of development of the productive forces these relations turn into their fetters. Then begins an epoch of social revolution" (quoted in Daum 1990). Every previous social system reached an end and the same will be true of capitalism.

Capital's powerful technology has become so vastly productive that it no longer fits within the confines of a system based on private ownership, class conflict, competition, and national borders—all of which developed to serve an economy of scarcity. Production for profit holds back the production of useful goods for all. Capitalism becomes less competitive; it revives older methods of non-market, statist, support; it returns to primitive accumulation. This epoch (and the phases within it) has been called by many names by various Marxists: the epoch of capitalist "decay," "decline," or "parasitism"; the epoch of "monopoly capitalism," "state monopoly capitalism," "imperialism," or "finance capitalism"; and sometimes simply "late capitalism." It is, as Marx put it, "an epoch of social revolution," or, as is sometimes asserted, "of wars and revolutions."

Of all the improvements in productivity, including automation, computers, and nanotechnology, the most significant invention that capitalism has created is the international working class itself. Before capitalism, there was no such class. It exists in concentrations in cities and in industries, working collectively and cooperatively (unlike peasants who generally work their own farms). In Marx's view, this class, with its hands on the highly productive new technology, could lead all the oppressed to create a new society, without classes, or states, or warfare, or ecological destruction. For over a century and a half, this modern working class has repeatedly, if intermittently, struggled, often under the banner of various sorts of "socialisms," to overthrow capitalism.

Marx and Engels did not live to see the actual epoch of capitalist decline (which began about 1900 or so). But various Marxist theorists analyzed it, including Hilferding, Lenin, Bukharin, Trotsky, and Luxemburg. All of them had important insights, although only Rosa Luxemburg was influential in the development of libertarian-democratic Marxist trends. However, I am going to stick as close as possible to the actual theories of Marx and Engels.

From 1914 through 1945, it was easy to believe that Marx had been correct in describing an epoch of capitalist decline. First, there was the historically unprecedented First World War. This was followed by the shallow prosperity of the twenties and then by the worldwide, decade-long, Great Depression. There were revolutions and near-revolutions throughout Europe. The Russian Revolution was the closest to being successful, but other revolutions failed in Germany, Italy, and Eastern Europe. There were major labor struggles in Europe and in the United States, as well as national rebellions, in China and elsewhere. Eventually, all the revolutionary struggles were defeated and replaced by totalitarian regimes. In the Soviet Union, Stalinism wiped out the last remnants of the Russian revolution (anarchists such as myself believe that it was Lenin and Trotsky who first betrayed the revolution by establishing a one-party police state). Fascism came to power in Italy, Germany, Spain, and other countries. Even slavery was revived, as a state measure, under Nazism and Stalinism. This initial phase of the epoch of decline culminated in the destructiveness of World War II. (I will discuss the subsequent phase, the postwar boom, in the next chapter.)

"Monopoly Capitalism"

What was the underlying nature of this phase of the epoch? Political economists took for granted the continuing reality of a competitive capitalism, where a large number of firms competed in a market and settled on the prices and rate of profit that the market enforced. Marx was one of the first to point out the drive of capitalist enterprises to grow larger and larger. He foresaw the growth of gigantic corporations due to "concentration and centralization."

"Concentration" is the ever increasing scale of accumulation of capital, into larger and larger firms. "Centralization" is the merger of separate capitals (capitalist businesses), either by amicable unions or by hostile takeovers of one by another.

> This splitting up of the total social capital into many individual capitals or the repulsion of its fractions one from another, is counteracted by their attraction. This last does not mean that simple concentration of the means of production and of the command over labor, which is identical with accumulation.... It is concentration of capitals already formed, destruction of their individual independence, expropriation of capitalist by capitalist, transformation of many small into few large capitals. This is centralization proper, as distinct from accumulation and concentration. (1906, 686–687)

This has clearly come to pass. As one example, Frances Moore Lappe writes, "Just four companies control at least three-quarters of the international grain trade; and in the United States, by 2000, just ten corporations—with boards totaling only 138 people—had come to account for half of US food and beverage sales" (2011, 11). Even a hundred and fifty years ago, Marx could see that the trend was toward the merger of all of a country's capital into a single entity, which would lay the basis for state capitalism. "This limit would not be reached in any particular society until the entire social capital would be united, either in the hands of one single capitalist, or in those of one single corporation" (Marx 1906, 688).

At the same time, this tendency is, as usual, complicated by counteracting forces. Mergers may not be consistent with technical needs (the merger was made for financial reasons, but the technologies of the different parts do not integrate well). In that case, giant capitals tend to break up into smaller ones, due to internal competitive forces, as different sub-businesses struggle to grow faster than the other sections—"the repulsion of its fractions one from another." Nor does the growth of huge firms end competition. Huge enterprises still compete with each other. Even monopolies compete with other monopolies (for example, a firm monopolizing aluminum might compete with a steel monopoly). Giant firms often find it useful to use smaller firms, for instance, in the way auto producers distribute through dealerships. New inventions arise that can force their way into the political economy (as personal computers did). And there are international firms: For decades no new US firm could break into the domination of the auto industry by GM, Ford, and Chrysler. Then, giant auto makers from Japan, Korea, and Germany (with backing by their states) were able to successfully compete with the former Big Three.

However, overall, and over time, the trend is toward increasing consolidation. This trajectory is what Lenin and others called "monopoly capitalism," though oligopoly (the rule of a few) capitalism might be a better name. Even if a small number of firms dominates a field, these semi-monopolies distort the forces of the market in a monopolistic manner (bourgeois economists call this "imperfect competition"). This includes distortion of the law of value (the tendency of commodities to exchange according to the amount of socially necessary labor they embody). *Nonetheless, distorted markets are still markets; distorted value relations are still value relations.*

Though it might seem strange to us today, Marx saw the growth of centralized big business as a mostly progressive development. He knew that it caused great suffering for the workers, but he also believed that it was building the technical and material basis for socialism (communism), the end of classes and poverty. We anarchists, on the other hand, historically had a more critical attitude toward the growth of big business. While agreeing that it might help lead to a cooperative, nonprofit, system of production, anarchists also understand that only *some* economic centralization is the result of more efficient technological methods of production. Firms also merge solely for financial reasons, or in order to increase their power over workers, or to have better access to markets. In a certain sense, the very process of monopolization itself can lead to less efficient outcomes by causing overcentralization, which interferes with production and distribution, and that holds back innovation (new inventions and new job creation are more likely to occur among smaller firms than larger ones). This view is consistent with an analysis of an epoch of capitalist decline. It is also consistent with the anarchists' goal of a socialized and cooperative economy within a radically democratic and decentralized federalism.

Effects of Oligopoly on the Capitalists

Some claim that Marx predicted that the growth of concentrated capital would erase the middle layers between the stock-owning bourgeoisie and the working class. This is not true. Marx did expect that small businesspeople, independent professionals, and small farmers would decline in numbers with the growth of big business. But he also predicted that huge firms would require splits between the ownership of capital and the job of managing the firm. "An industrial army of workmen, under the command of a capitalist, requires, like a real army, officers (managers), and sergeants (foremen, overlookers).... The work of supervision becomes their established and exclusive function" (1906, 364). This results in the "...development of a numerous class of industrial and commercial managers..." (1967b, 389). As capitalist enterprises expand, the capitalists themselves become superfluous, at least to the productive aspects. The managers manage. The capitalists invest in the stock market.

This new layer of managers and supervisors has basically two tasks. One is the technical coordination of the various tasks taking place. This is something that would have to be done in any economic system. Under socialist democracy, it might be done collectively by workers meeting to plan their work, or the workers might elect a coordinator, or they might take turns at the job. To the extent that capitalist managers do necessary technical work, they are part of the collective labor that produces the commodities. On the other hand, they are agents of the capitalists and personifications of capital. Their job is to drive the wage slaves to their labors and make sure the workers do not "goof off." Supervisors may have interests that clash with the capitalist owners (it is a very conflictual system), but workers tend to see them as part of the class enemy.

For Marx, the replacement of family-owned and managed firms by ever-larger stock companies points to the end of capitalism, its last phase. "This is the abolition of the capitalist mode of production within the capitalist mode of production itself…. It establishes a monopoly in certain spheres and therefore requires state interference. It reproduces a new financial aristocracy, a new variety of parasites…a whole system of swindling and cheating by means of corporation promotion, stock issuance, and stock speculation." (1967b, 438). He thought that the growth of monopolies would result in more state involvement in the economy as well as the growth of finance and speculation. He was right.

Effects of Oligopoly on the Working Class

Another frequent misinterpretation of Marx involves his supposed "theory of immiseration"—the idea that the growth of big business would directly result in increasing poverty among the working class. This is a misrepresentation of his "general law of capitalist accumulation." Remember: All of Marx's "laws" are "tendencies," which work their effects in the face of counteracting tendencies. He did not think that all workers would be automatically driven to extreme poverty. He knew that they could be relatively well-paid, while still being exploited, and he expected that workers would earn more during periods of prosperity in the business cycle.

Capitalists constantly push down on workers' standard of living and the workers push back. For a period, this evolves into a relatively stable value of the commodity labor power. But the capitalists will continue to press the workers, especially when profit rates decline—and when the bosses feel stronger due to increased centralization. Increased productivity permits the capitalists to preserve or even lower the value of what they pay the workers, while maintaining their standard of living as judged by use-values. This lasts until the crisis gets so bad, the profit rate gets so low, that the capitalists have to attack the workers and drastically cut their wages.

Workers fight back to maintain their standard of living—and, if possible, to improve it. This is important for them to do, Marx noted, but in itself, it does not directly challenge capitalist exploitation as such.

> Just as little as better clothing, food and treatment…do away with the exploitation of the slave, so little do they set aside that of the wage worker. A rise in the price of labor…only means, in fact, that the length and weight of the golden chain the wage worker has already forged for himself, allow of a relaxation of the tension of it…. The condition of [labor power's] sale, whether more or less favorable to the laborer, include therefore the necessity of its constant re-selling. (1906, 677–678)

As capitalist accumulation and centralization increase, the workers' wages may go up or down. However, their domination by the ever-increasing power of the capitalists (their alienation) worsens. Meanwhile, increasing productivity (the increasing organic composition of capital) continues to decrease the proportion of human labor needed in production. People lose jobs, which expands the reserve army of the unemployed. *The poverty and misery of the unemployed does get worse over time*, and threatens to pull down the standards of even the organized, employed workers. "In proportion as capital accumulates, the lot of *the laborer, be his payment high or low,* must grow worse…. This law rivets the laborer to capital" (Marx 1906, 708–709; my emphasis).

Oligopoly and the Rate of Profit

How does oligopoly—or even complete unification in the form of state capitalism—affect the tendency of the rate of profit to fall? Clearly, productivity continues to increase, which raises the organic composition of capital, which should decrease the rate of profit. But does it?

Monopoly and oligopoly interfere with the average rate of profit. Giant firms can raise their prices (and, therefore, profits), without worrying that other capitalists will invest in their field and bring them back down. Because of their monopoly position, they can keep out other possible competitors, which is what makes their position a monopoly in the first place. Their monopoly position may be due to ownership of patents or to their huge size. It takes a great deal of capital to break into many US industries, which is why it often takes large foreign companies to do it. So, the giant firms may get and keep a disproportionate amount of the surplus value produced in society. Which means that the weaker, smaller firms are getting proportionately less (the extra surplus value has to come from somewhere). However, this does not change the total amount of surplus value produced by society's collective body of workers.

Concentrated and centralized big businesses also produce large amounts of surplus in one place. While the rate of profit may not be high, the lump sum of any one corporation might be quite large. This does not change the actual rate of profit, but it does change the effects of the declining rate of profit. A large, concentrated sum of money can be used for further investment in a way that the same sum of money, scattered around in small firms, cannot.

Large firms may also increase profits through economies of scale in production. However, as anarchists and other decentralists (Borsodi 1933; Sale 1980; Schumacher 1973; and others) have argued, there are also diseconomies of scale that are rarely looked at. For example, a centralized factory that produces all the widgets in the world may produce them much cheaper than would local widget-making workshops. But the factory would have to import raw materials, machinery, and workers from great distances, and then to ship the finished widgets great distances. This creates costs that local production would not have. These diseconomies of scale can become a factor in the splitting up of overlarge monopolies. Whether the costs of distribution balance the advantages of centralized production has to be determined empirically, but rarely is. In the 1930s, the decentralist Ralph Borsodi calculated that two-thirds of goods were made more cheaply locally, with small machines, than on a national scale (1933). Of course, technology has changed a great deal since then, and he did not calculate for regional production, but his findings remain telling.

Monopolies and semi-monopolies are also, as mentioned, under less competitive pressure and therefore may be less inventive and productive. Monopolies tend to stagnate. On the one hand, this produces less surplus value. On the other hand, slowing growth in productivity also slows the growth of the organic composition of capital and therefore of the fall in the rate of profit. How this balances out is another empirical matter. But in the long run, the fall in the rate of profit cannot really be counteracted by the effects of stagnation.

However, the most important consequence of the growth of large, concentrated firms for profit rates is its effect on the business cycle. If a cycle goes all the way through to the final crash (as it did in 1929), the crash will be very bad indeed under oligopolistic capitalism. Huge businesses have huge falls. They owe huge debts to other companies and to the banks. They employ large numbers of workers. They buy and sell from each other and from many smaller firms. Their boards of directors overlap. So if any of them fall, the effect on the whole of the economy is enormous. The problem of getting an oligopolistic economy back up on its feet is also enormous. While classical bourgeois economists claim that an economic slump will always cure itself, Keynes argued that this was no longer automatically true. In the age of monopolies, he was right. The Great Depression lasted for ten years, and almost 20 percent of the US workforce was still unemployed when a world war finally ended it.

That is why the capitalist class and its economists and politicians are determined not to let another Great Depression happen. The corporations and banks are just "too big to fail," or rather, too big to be *allowed* to fail. Governments and central banks will do all they can to prevent another Depression. The usual methods are economic stimuli and subsidies, tax cuts, and monetary maneuvers that decrease interest rates.

Assuming these methods work, at least for a while, they may not completely banish the business cycle and its crashes, but they may modulate them, make them less disastrous. However, this has an unintended consequence. Smaller downturns cannot perform their historical task of cleaning up the capitalist economy. Without big crashes, inefficient businesses may not go bankrupt; inefficient parts of monopolistic combinations may stay in business (as opposed to becoming "lean and mean"); neither the costs of materials nor wage levels will decline as much; debts will not be written off but will continue to accumulate. If the costs of doing business do not decline, the rate of profit does not get a boost to counteract its tendency to fall. The shallowness of the business cycle in the 1950s—a cycle that bourgeois economists were so proud of—was preparing the way for greater disasters.

Not-So-Primitive Accumulation

Increasing wealth by non-market, or at least non-value-producing, methods never stopped, even at the height of capitalist development. Now, it has returned with a vengeance. Since it is no longer "primitive" or "primary," theorists sometimes use other terms; David Harvey (2010) prefers "accumulation by dispossession," for example. Whatever we call them, these "new" forms of accumulation all involve the theft (legal or otherwise) of things that were once common property, someone else's property, or that had never previously been considered property at all. It turns all sorts of previously unsalable, unmarketable, things into commodities. This includes privatization of public industries, privatization of natural resources (such as water), the whole process of de-nationalization of the former "Communist" countries (turning the economy over to traditional capitalists, often former bureaucrats), the stripping of assets from weaker corporations, efforts to patent genetic material, continuing efforts to drive people off the land in China and elsewhere, and much more.

Taken as a whole, the ruling class acts like the capitalist management of a global firm that sells its commodities for the equivalent of variable capital, constant capital, and the average profit. Prudent management would dictate that, after selling its commodities, it should put aside money from the equivalent of the constant capital to eventually pay for new machinery and buildings when the old ones wear out. But it does not. It makes its bottom-line look healthier by counting the value that should have gone toward replacing constant capital as part of its profit. Or it uses some of the constant capital value to buy off the workers with higher pay (thus, counting it as variable capital). The day will come when its machinery will wear out. Then this seemingly prosperous firm will fail because it cannot replace the machines. It will have to dig even deeper to come up with new sources of profit.

The looting of nature is one crucial result of this shortsightedness. Constant capital is not just machines; it includes raw materials as well. In a global economy based mostly on nonrenewable resources, the bourgeoisie also should have been putting aside wealth to prepare for a transition from oil, coal, and natural gas to renewable energy. It should have been paying to clean up the environment and preventing global warming. Instead it has been counting its wealth as profit and buying off a layer of the working class with a standard of living decent enough to obscure the looming catastrophe.

Our whole civilization is built on carbon-based fuels. Not only our transportation system, but also our food, which relies on artificial fertilizer and artificial pesticides made from oil. And there are all the things we use made from plastics and artificial fibers (also made from oil). These are limited, nonrenewable, raw materials that sooner or later will run out—and in the meantime, they get harder and harder to extract. They pollute our foods, our land, our air, and our water. They are causing global warming. And the drive to accumulate leads capitalists to make matters worse every day. The world's forests (the "lungs of the earth") are being destroyed. The oceans are being overfished to extinction. Other species are being wiped out. Capitalism treats the world as though it were an inexhaustible mine.

Marx and Engels did not foresee all this; they expected a socialist revolution well before humanity got this close to the edge. But their tools help us to understand it, to see beyond the surface. For instance, sometimes, when gasoline prices go up, liberals claim that the oil companies are deliberately overpricing it. This may be immediately true, but in the long run, it is not. Because the oil companies do not include the costs they will eventually need in order to reach hard-to-get oil or to develop new energy sources once current oil sources run low, they are all underpricing the real costs of oil production. When conservatives claim that changing to renewable energy and an ecologically sustainable economy would be difficult and expensive; they are absolutely correct.

Imperialism: The Stolen Wealth of Nations

For reasons known only to himself, Lenin gave the name "imperialism" to the epoch of late capitalism. Of course, imperialism goes back at least to the Roman and Chinese empires, and *capitalist* imperialism begins with the very foundations of capitalism, with the British, Spanish, and French empires, among others.

Marx wrote a fair amount about the imperialism of his time in his political writings and anthropological notebooks—especially about the British rule over India, China, and Ireland, the Dutch rule over Indonesia, the

Russian rule over Poland, and the French attempt to conquer Mexico. But he did not write much about its economics. In a more general sense, he saw foreign trade by the industrializing capitalist countries of Western Europe as an essential background to their development. Driven by the need to make profits, the original industrial capitalist regimes went abroad to exploit the labor force, the raw materials, and the consumer markets of poorer nations.

In the *Communist Manifesto*, Marx declares of the bourgeoisie, "The cheap prices of its commodities are the heavy artillery with which it batters down all Chinese walls…. It compels all nations, on pain of extinction, to adopt the bourgeois mode of production; it compels them to introduce what it calls civilization into their midst, i.e., to become bourgeois themselves….It has made barbarian and semi-barbarian countries dependent on the civilized ones, nations of peasants on nations of bourgeois, the East on the West" (in Draper 1998, 115–117; note both the archaic use of "barbarian" and the critical reference to bourgeois society as "what it calls civilization"). Capital in the developed countries would take advantage of cheaper labor and the higher levels of exploitation in the poor nations.

Such directly capitalist methods have always been tied up with primitive accumulation, the looting of local peoples of their wealth by force and fraud. Although formal colonialism (the ownership of other countries by the imperial home countries) is mostly over, the looting continues, through investments, high-interest loans to governments (including by the IMF and the World Bank), unequal trade, control over international patents, etc.

In light of all this, Marx's attitude toward early capitalist imperialism was ambivalent. On one hand, he saw it as laying the basis for industrialization and modernization in the poorer nations, a way to break them out of what he saw as the "stagnation" of pre-capitalist societies. Yet he was aware of the suffering that capitalist imperialism caused among ordinary people, the destruction of traditional ways of life. He was sympathetic to anti-imperialist rebellions, as in India, China, and Mexico. While some of what he wrote seems to imply that every nation must necessarily pass through a "capitalist stage" before achieving socialism, he later qualified this by claiming that a pre-capitalist society could skip that stage *provided that* it was helped by proletarian revolutions in the industrialized countries. Today it is clear that once capitalism reaches its epoch of decay, imperialism is a completely reactionary phenomena.

There are various contemporary Marxist theories of imperialism, which I will not review here. Suffice it to say that the giant oligopolies of the rich countries dominate the world market, driven by the need to make profits and accumulate value. As such, they also dominate the poorer, oppressed, countries, in order to drain them of their wealth. To maintain their power, the capitalists of the imperialist nations can use the military forces of their national states to threaten, bomb, and even invade or occupy the weaker countries. Implicitly, they also use them to warn off rival imperialist states. This is most true for the rulers of the United States.

Competition among imperial states has meant repeated wars throughout the history of capitalism. They have developed weapons of such awesome power that they could wipe out civilization and perhaps exterminate life on earth. The alleged deterrent power of these nuclear and biological weapons did not prevent many smaller wars by the imperialists against oppressed nations. Now that the Cold War is over and the Soviet Union as such is gone, nuclear bombs are more widespread than ever. They are under the control of more, often unstable, governments, as well as the increasingly desperate imperialist states: an extremely dangerous situation for human survival.

Real Democracy

The epoch of capitalist decline has political effects. At its birth, the ideologues of capitalism developed the program of bourgeois-democracy. It was based on the nature of capitalism itself. All people were supposedly equal, free atoms in the marketplace and therefore they should be free and equal citizens under the state. When buying and selling in the market, people's race, religion, gender, family background, country of origin, etc. do not matter; all that matters is how much money they have (a quantitative, not a qualitative, difference). Similarly, all citizens should be equal, with one (adult) person, one vote. "An inalienable right to life, liberty, and the pursuit of happiness." "Liberty, equality, and fraternity." This implied freedom of speech, the press, and association. It meant election of officials, land to the peasants, and national self-determination. There should be no oppression or discrimination based on anything but lack of money.

Of course, capitalism has never lived up to its promised program. Every expansion of democratic rights was won by the blood of the people fighting the capitalists, even the most basic freedoms were concessions forced upon the ruling class. But those rights did expand: The right to vote was won in country after country; absolute monarchies were replaced by either republics or, at least, constitutional monarchies; women's rights were expanded; slavery was abolished.

But Marx understood that the struggle would become more intense over time, that the growth of capitalism would lead to a decline in capitalism's own democratic program. The expansion of capitalism meant the expansion of the working class. The bourgeoisie became more afraid of the growing proletariat than they were of undemocratic, authoritarian rulers. From the very beginning, the emerging capitalist rulers knew that a successful revolution against the feudal aristocracy might turn into one against the bourgeoisie. Democracy itself might be used by the workers to organize themselves against the capitalist class. And their fears were well founded. While bourgeois forms of representative democracy have often successfully contained and channeled worker unrest, in its epoch of decline, capitalism increasingly ceases to be a champion of even bourgeois democracy. It is becoming ever more obvious that, for democratic rights to be secured, the working class must overthrow capitalism totally and create a true democracy, a socialist democracy.

And this has always been necessary. Marx and Engels (and most anarchists) understood that the rising, semi-autonomous bourgeois state, with its bureaucratic-military executive, served capitalism overall, even when it was not directly controlled by the capitalist class. They called this trend "Bonapartism," after the dictatorship of Napoleon and later of his nephew, but applied it to other states as well. In their *Address of the Central Committee to the Communist League (March 1850)*, Marx and Engels drew the lessons they had learned from the defeat of the 1848–1850 European revolutions. They concluded that the workers should support the liberal democrats against authoritarian states, but never trust them; they will sell out the struggle for fear of the working class. The workers should organize independently of the bourgeoisie, even of its most liberal wing. They should push to go all the way, to workers' rule and the beginning of socialism, as the only way to achieve even the limited claims of bourgeois democracy: They concluded, "*Their battle-cry must be: The Permanent Revolution*" (Marx 1973, 330).

By "permanent," they meant "uninterrupted," "going all the way," "not stopping at any stage." Only a total revolution, by the working class and its allies among all the oppressed, could go all the way to a socialist democracy. The replacement of capitalism and the bourgeois state by an association of workers' councils and popular committees would be the only way to complete the democratic and libertarian promises of the bourgeois-democratic revolutions.

Chapter 5: The Post-War Boom and Fictitious Capital

AFTER the Second World War, most economists predicted a return to depression conditions. This included most bourgeois economists as well as almost all Marxist economists. But it did not happen. Instead a new period of prosperity began, sometimes even called the "Golden Age" of capitalism, which lasted for about twenty to thirty years (from the end of the 'forties to about 1970).

During this post-war period, there was relatively high employment. In the United States, most (white) working families had houses and cars, and usually only the husband had to work. Their children had access to higher education and the country enjoyed a so-called "labor peace" between management and the unions in big industries. In apparent contradiction to the theory of permanent revolution, which would have predicted a steady decline in democratic rights, fascism was overcome in Europe (except for Spain and Portugal) and bourgeois democracy restored. Increasing numbers of colonized nations won their political independence. To most people, any notion of capitalism being in decline seemed preposterous. The only enemy appeared to be totalitarian "Communist" Russia.

Still, from the perspective of the ruling class, some problems remained. On a world scale, capitalism was still unable to industrialize the poorer nations. Even the

Western European countries took many years after the war to rebuild their prosperity. "Communist" and nationalist revolutions continued in the poor countries (especially China, Korea, Vietnam, Yugoslavia, and Cuba) and Italy and France had large "Communist" parties. The imperialist countries continued to get into colonial wars (the biggest for the United States being in Korea and Vietnam). As mentioned, nuclear weapons grew in number and destructive power.

In the United States, there were still many pockets of poverty: the "Other America." The South was impoverished and held back by its vicious anti-Black laws. Unions abandoned their efforts to organize that part of the country. Millions of African-Americans lived under a form of totalitarian repression. A right-wing, anti-communist, hysteria swept the nation, driving leftists out of the unions, out of colleges, and out of other places of employment. It attacked freedom of speech and association. The economy as a whole still went through business cycles, from boom to bust, even if in a shallower, more moderate, fashion than before.

Causes of the Post-War Prosperity

If capitalism was (and is) in its epoch of decline, then what caused this post-World War II boom, however limited? Did it disprove Marx's theory? The short answer is that *what the Great Depression could not do sufficiently to restore capitalism to apparent health, the world war could do.*

As I have said, economic downturns function to "clear the slate" by reducing economic values. The Depression could not do enough to destroy the values of constant capital. The world war, on the other hand, destroyed constant capital itself—factories, machines, roads, buildings, and raw materials went up in flames all across Europe and Asia. This meant they could be rebuilt after the war with the most modern, productive, technology. Similarly, the value of variable capital—the commodity labor power—went down with the massacres and social destruction of the war around the world. It took decades for the educated and skilled workers of Europe to regain their pre-World War I standard of living. In this case, though, capitalism had also benefited from years of working class defeats, from the twenties onward, of failures to make revolutions, and of successful counterrevolutions, with the horrors of Nazism and Stalinism. That culminated in the period right after World War II, when social democratic and Stalinist parties kept working class struggles everywhere within the limits of capitalism.

Yet the Western ruling classes had certain limitations due to the potential power of the working classes. The capitalists did not want to see a revival of revolutionary class consciousness, as had happened after World War I. They preferred to control the workers through bourgeois democracies rather than revive fascism. There were large unions in Europe and a third of the US private sector workers were in unions. Since they could not simply crush the workers again, as in fascism, the Western capitalists permitted a rise in the standard of living for the workers and increased social benefits (the "welfare state")—for the time being.

The US economy was pumped up through the massive stimulus of military spending, far more than the New Deal had ever attempted. The state took wealth from all of society and concentrated it into the hands of a few "centralized and concentrated" semi-monopolies. High levels of military spending continued after the war, both of conventional armed forces and of nuclear-armed missiles and bombers. President Dwight Eisenhower was to call this the "military-industrial complex," and some Marxists called it the "Permanent Arms Economy." It was also referred to as "military Keynesianism."

Concentration was increased on a world scale as international imperialism was reorganized. The British empire (and the lesser French, Dutch, etc., empires) was essentially superseded by the hegemonic rule of US capital. The dollar became the dominant world currency.

In the United States the prosperity included an expansion of debt and speculation, particularly in the fields of FIRE (finance, insurance, and real estate). Meanwhile there was an explosion of the automobile industry, which expanded the steel, rubber, and glass industries, highway construction, and resulted in the construction of suburbia.

These forces countered the long-run tendencies of stagnation and decline. They did not run out of steam until the middle of the 1960s. From 1970 to the mid-70s, the world capitalist economy began to slide downhill again (with ups and downs), deeper into stagnation. A new attack on the working class became necessary.

The Limits of the Post-War Boom

Liberals wondered, if the state could spend so much money on war and preparing for war, why not get the same economic effect by spending on socially useful causes like universal healthcare, education, environmental protection, housing for the homeless, and so on? They called, in effect, for a "new New Deal."

In the most abstract sense, this could have been done. Western European countries, which had influential social democratic or "Communist" parties, provide more and better social services than the United States does—starting with universal health coverage—within the limits of capitalism. However, there are class reasons why the capitalist state cannot provide vast funds for social purposes. Even in Western Europe, social services have been under fierce attack for some time, although they still enjoy more benefits than the US population ever has.

Quite simply, the capitalist class will not hand a large chunk of its collective profits (total surplus value) over to the working class. This would both cut down overall profit and politically strengthen the workers. With more social support to fall back on, workers might be more willing to strike and to demand higher pay. Socially useful products provided by the state, such as houses, food, and medical care, would compete on the market with the same commodities made by private capitalists. Ideologically, if the people saw that the state could provide extensive benefits and produce needed products, they might think, "Why do we need the capitalists?" Workers might start thinking in terms of some sort of socialism. This would not do, from the viewpoint of the bourgeoisie. This is not why they have a bourgeois state.

Some sorts of government spending, on the other hand, are completely acceptable. Military spending, for instance, is a direct state subsidy to big capitalists. It does not compete on the market place (no one makes nuclear missiles for private sale, at least not legally). It channels value to some of the biggest corporations. It has its own ideological justification ("defense") that protects it when politicians cut social benefits for workers and the poor.

I am focusing on the economic effects of military spending, but I do not deny that it does have its uses for the empire. The United States does need materiel in order to invade smaller countries. Even nuclear missiles are supposedly useful for deterring nuclear attacks from enemies, although this reaches crazy thinking (since any use of such "weapons" would destroy both the attacker and the defender). The economic basis of military spending become obvious every time the government considers adding new weapons or retiring old ones. The companies that make them throw their lobbyists into high gear. They whip up the workers who make these products to demonstrate and petition. The politicians representing the regions where armaments are manufactured—whose re-election campaigns are financed by these same companies—demand continued support for the industry and the ideology behind it.

But military spending has an inherent weakness. When tractors, for example, are produced, they can be used by farmers to grow things. Bulldozers can be used in the next production cycle to make buildings. But what about tanks? Once manufactured, the tanks either stay at home, producing nothing, or they are sent abroad, where they destroy things. This is even more true for intercontinental nuclear missiles. Much value goes into making them, but they are not to be used, and hopefully will never be. Whatever its political or military significance, military spending is economically the same as paying capitalists to hire workers to dig big holes and fill them in again.

Suppose the government decides to make some missiles. It has a fund of money, some from taxes (ultimately from the pool of surplus value) and most from borrowing (selling bonds, a range of Treasury Department securities; the government takes in money from its buyers and promises to repay the cost of the bonds with a certain amount of profit at a future date). It pays a capitalist firm to make them (including what the firm counts as profit). The firm buys necessary material (constant capital), such as steel and machines. The firm hires workers (variable capital) to make the missiles. At the end of this process the government has gone deeper into debt, but (1) the buyers of the government bonds count themselves as having new wealth, (2) the firm has profits that it pays out to its stockholders and/or saves for further investment, (3) the workers have their wages, which they spend on consumer goods, health care, and sending their children to college. BUT while all this paper (bonds, stocks in the arms company, money) has increased and continues to circulate, there are no new products on the market! Marx called this circulating paper wealth "fictitious value" or, when used as capital, "fictitious capital."

It is sick enough to think of an economic system that sustains itself (in large part) by preparing for mass nuclear death. It is even sicker to have an economy that sustains itself by effectively producing... nothing. This *is* the epoch of capitalist decay.

Fictitious Capital

What are those treasury bonds exactly? They are past loans to the state, loans made by the people, companies, or governments who purchase the bonds. The government quickly spends that money; it is quite literally no longer there. So what the bond-holders own, according to Marx, are "paper duplicates of consumed capital" that entitle them to a portion of future tax revenue (1967b, 477). While "real capital" exists in the form of actual commodities, machines, and the like, "fictitious capital" exists only as an idea, a promise.

Arms production and other forms of public expenditure are not the only way to create fictitious capital. When housing prices rise in a housing bubble, despite the fact that no new wealth has been created, this is fictitious capital. When oil is produced and revenue is not set aside for the future to pay for reaching hard-to-get oil, the profit claimed is fictitious capital. Rent of land that has not been improved by human labor is fictitious capital. Wealth created by primary accumulation is fictitious capital. Speculation on stocks and bonds, with increasingly remote relations to the real economy they supposedly represent is fictitious capital.

Complex financial "instruments," so complex that even those who design them have difficulty understanding what they really measure, are fictitious capital.

As Marx describes it,

> Titles of ownership to public works, railways, mines, etc., are...titles to real capital. But they do not place this capital at one's disposal. It is not subject to withdrawal. They merely convey legal claims to a portion of the surplus-value to be produced by it. But these titles likewise become paper duplicates of the real capital; it is as though a bill of lading were to acquire a value separate from the cargo, both concomitantly and simultaneously with it. They come to nominally represent non-existent capital. For the real capital exists side by side with them and does not change hands as a result of the transfer of these duplicates from one person to another. (ibid, 477–478)

The result is an incoherent mess that masks what is really going on in the economy "Everything here appears distorted, since in this paper world, the real price and its real basis appear nowhere, but only bullion, metal coin, notes, bill of exchange, securities…. The entire process becomes incomprehensible" (ibid, 490).

During times of prosperity, people take for granted that the paper wealth represents real wealth and can be turned into real wealth whenever needed. Meanwhile, the paper or blips on a computer screen is bought and sold, exchanged and rearranged, making everything look prosperous and profitable, despite the stagnation in the real economy. In fact, when the profit rates of the real economy stagnate or decline (due to the falling rate of profit and the growth of monopoly) there is more pressure to make money by investing in ever more fictitious capital in the form of loans and exotic derivatives. Eventually, the entire economy becomes "financialized."

In an economic downturn, there is suddenly a dash to turn the paper into real products, or at least to make sure that they do represent real commodities: gold or houses or machinery. The need for goods and services that have been produced by socially-necessary labor reasserts itself, as the economy shifts from fictitious value to real value, and people discover there is much less of the latter than they thought. As in a game of musical chairs, many capitalists have nowhere to sit.

A big crash, at the end of a business cycle, clears away a lot of fictitious capital. But the long prosperity we are currently coming out of depended on a variety of tricks that modulated the cycle to prevent such crashes. Therefore, the amount of fictitious capital—of debt and financial speculative instruments—has grown to mountainous proportions, in both governmental and private forms. The pressure on the system simultaneously grows for a real, big crash to re-stabilize the system.

Unproductive Consumption

Marx divided the productive economy roughly into what he called Department I (which produces constant capital) and Department II (which produces consumer goods). Department II provides for the working class (variable capital), which need food, housing, healthcare, and entertainment in order to reenter the cycle of production—that is, to go to work the next day.

Capitalists also consume commodities, of course. However, their gourmet meals, mansions, and yachts are luxuries. They do not re-enter the cycle of production, because capitalists are not necessary for production. Marx treated their consumption as a sliver of Department II, as "unproductive consumption" (Marx 1967a). Productive consumption uses up goods in the process of producing surplus value, while the capitalists' unproductive consumption of luxuries is paid for entirely out of the capitalist's revenue, using up surplus value, not creating it. The middle layers of society—managers, supervisors, bureaucrats—mostly work for the capitalists (directly or indirectly) and are paid out of already existing value; they do not create new surplus value.

Arms spending and similar forms of wasteful production have exponentially expanded this "luxury" production. Government arms production, fictitious capital, new forms of primitive accumulation, and financialization kept capitalism going after World War II. The apparent prosperity lasted for about thirty years. It has been downhill since then, and it is getting worse. The underlying tendencies of the epoch of capitalist decay are reasserting themselves. That is what we are now living through and will continue to live through, I believe, until there is either a collapse of civilization or a working class-led revolution.

Understanding the post-war boom in general is no substitute for an analysis of the current economic crisis. Nor can it precisely predict the future, on any set schedule. It does, however, show that the period of apparent prosperity does not contradict Marx's concept of the epoch of capitalist decay, and that his concept of fictitious capital is important for understanding the world today.

Chapter 6: State Capitalism

AS we have seen, Marx described a tendency of capitalism to develop, despite all counteracting tendencies, larger and larger firms. The trends toward centralization and concentration were due to accumulation (growing larger), competition (some firms beating other firms and absorbing them), the class struggle (getting larger in order to better dominate the workers), and the use of credit and fictitious capital, among other factors. Monopolization and the giant firms it required caused increasing intervention by the state in the economy. The overall trend, Marx noted, was toward a single, merged, firm, though he did not say whether he expected this trend to ever be completed. Even a single national firm, however, would still be capitalist. It would compete with other giant firms and, as Marx suggests, "Where the state itself is a capitalist producer, as in the exploitation of mines, forests, etc., its product is a 'commodity' and hence possesses the specific character of every other commodity" (quoted in Kliman 2012, 210).

Engels's Concept of State Capitalism

Marx's close friend and collaborator, Frederick Engels, further elaborated this idea of a trend toward a unified, state-run, capitalism. Engels was especially impressed by the rise of "trusts," business entities by which all the companies in an industry, on a national or international level, agreed to divide up a market and set prices. In fact though, since trusts were based on distinct companies that got stronger or weaker over time, they tended to eventually break up. They did not have the staying power of today's multinational corporations. This led Engels to imagine another possible conclusion for the trend.

> The official representative of capitalist society—the state—will ultimately have to undertake the direction of production....The transformation of the great establishments for production and distribution into joint-stock companies, trusts, and state property show how unnecessary the bourgeoisie are.... All the social functions of the capitalist are now performed by salaried employees. The capitalist has no further social function than that of pocketing dividends, tearing off coupons, and gambling on the Stock Exchange....
>
> But the transformation, either into joint-stock companies and trusts, or into state ownership, does not do away with the capitalistic nature of the productive forces....The modern state, no matter what its form, is essentially a capitalist machine, the state of the capitalists, the ideal personification of the total national capital. The more it proceeds to the taking over the productive forces, the more does it actually become the national capitalist, the more citizens does it exploit. The workers remain wage-workers—proletarians. The capitalist relation is not done away with. It is rather brought to a head. But brought to a head, it topples over. (Engels 1954, 384–386)

Engels was saying that the logical endpoint of corporations, trusts, and monopolies, is state capitalism, although he never actually uses the term (it could just as well be called "statified capitalism"). Like Marx, he also never said whether he expected this to actually happen or was just describing a tendency. (Marx had read through this discussion by Engels and expressed no disagreement.)

As he described state capitalism, the economy is managed by salaried employees, bureaucrats, officials, and managers. They are the state and as such the personification of capital. That is, they would exploit the workers in a capitalist fashion (as opposed to the methods of feudalism, or slavery, or of some new class society). He expected that the bourgeoisie would continue to exist, living as stock-owning parasites, but not actually managing anything.

By contrast, Bakunin predicted that a completely state-run economy would develop a new ruling class from better-paid workers and socialist intellectuals. In their writing on the "Asiatic mode of production" and other aspects of pre-capitalist society, Marx and Engels discussed societies where the means of production, especially land, had been owned by the state and collectively ruled by bureaucratic classes. They did not, however, make any connection between this and capitalist statification. This may have been because they felt that these societies (for example, some of the Central American "Indian" empires) were virtually stagnant, lacking any real drive to accumulate, and thus had little in common with capitalism.

Under state capitalism, there will still be proletarians—not slaves, not serfs, but proletarians. They will be selling their labor power to the collective capitalist, the state, and will work to produce commodities, more commodities than their labor power is worth. In other words, they will continue to produce surplus value. Engels did not comment on how competition might continue internationally—among capitalist states or between them and other monopolistic businesses. His key point is that the capital/labor relationship continues. That is what makes state capitalism capitalist.

State Capitalism in Reality

What was for Marx and Engels more of a logical trend has long been observable in the real world. Historically, capitalist governments have owned railroads and other productive enterprises, even automobile factories or coal mines. Even now, when the right-wing, anti-Keynesians have won hegemony over economic discourse, statism remains strong. Despite all the talk about "free-markets" and "liberty," the rightists have not called for ending state subsidies to the armament and other industries. In fact, they champion increased police and military power for the state.

But examples of complete statification did not come through the merger of traditional capitalist monopolies, as Engels had imagined. It came through Marxist-Leninist-led revolutions in Russia, China, Cuba, and other countries, and later with the expansion of the Soviet Union's military power into eastern Europe. In these countries, weak bourgeoisies were overthrown, but the working class was unable to take or maintain power. As a result, the actual state capitalist systems that did develop differed from Engels's model in certain ways. The lingering, parasitical bourgeoisie he postulated was wiped out (even though a small number of capitalists filtered back into the new state bureaucracies). And the system covered itself in a pseudo-socialist, semi-Marxist ideology, to justify itself and to confuse the population.

However, as Engels (and Bakunin) had described, actual power resided in a layer of "salaried employees," a collectivist bureaucracy. They "owned" the state property, in the sense that, collectively, they could do what they wanted with it—which is what ownership is. Collectively, they held "private property," in the sense that it was kept "private" (separate) from the mass of the population. Individual bureaucrats lived far better than did ordinary workers. They could not directly pass on their property to their children (leaving aside the bizarre dictatorship in North Korea!), but, by education and contacts, their children were guaranteed places in the bureaucracy.

The state remained a capitalist state, a bureaucratic-military-centralized instrument of capital accumulation.

Not only was the total state capital of these countries in competition on the world market, but it was internally divided into competing entities and commodity market-places. The workers remained proletarians, selling their labor power for money on a labor market (there was a great deal of labor turnover), producing surplus value, producing commodities, and buying commodities on the consumer market (as did the capitalist bureaucrats).

Farmers worked at collective farms (officially cooperatives, not state farms) that sold goods on the markets.
They also usually had small private plots where they
raised produce to sell. The large enterprises also sold
means of production to each other (using contracts and
bank accounts); therefore means of production were also
commodities. And the whole thing was held together by
gray and black markets, deal making, and trading. There
was usually an official economic "plan," but it was never
actually fulfilled.

The economies of the Soviet Union and Maoist China
were highly distorted and deformed forms of capitalism,
where the laws of capitalism operated in an indirect and
mediated way. But *a distorted market is still a market and a
distorted capitalism is still capitalism*. Think, for instance,
of capitalism under Nazi totalitarianism or the historical
US "company towns." The "Communist" countries had,
despite all the window dressing, capitalist economies.

Just as much as any corporation, the Soviet Union was
driven to accumulate. In fact, its growth during the 1930s
and 1940s was often cited as proof of its "socialist" nature.
But just as much as capitalist business firms, the USSR
was driven to accumulate. This was the historic task of the
capitalist class, in any of its forms, as it ground down the
working class.

Engels did not expect such societies to last long.
"Brought to a head, it topples over." Marx had emphasized
how units of capital (companies) that were overcentral-
ized for their level of technical productivity would fly
apart, dissolving into smaller units, as a result of internal

competitive pressures, but Engels tended to emphasize the political effects. Writing about the monopolistic power of the trusts, he wrote that "the exploitation is so palpable that it must break down. No nation will put up with production conducted by trusts, with so barefaced an exploitation of the community by a small band of dividend mongers" (1954, 384). In the Soviet Union, this effect was countered for a time by the absence of a traditional, propertied, bourgeoisie and the effective use of ideology to mask the true nature of social relationships.

For whatever reason, Marx and Engels saw state capitalism as ultimately fragile. It was, and remains, unable to solve the basic problems of capitalism, including its tendencies toward eventual stagnation, increasing conflict between capitalists and proletarians, and an explosive, crisis-ridden economy. In fact, the statified and collectivized form of capitalism that once existed in the Soviet Union and China did break down. Given the weaknesses of the world working classes at the time, unfortunately what replaced it was a more traditional form of capitalism (with a great deal of state involvement). But there is no inherent reason that state capitalisms cannot appear again under certain conditions—such as the defeat of a working class revolution.

The question of whether or not the Soviet Union and Nazi Germany had the "same" economic system is an interesting one. Without going into detail, I will say that they were both capitalist economies with a great deal of merger between the state and the economy (consistent with Marx and Engels's expected trends). The ruling totalitarian parties dominated their national economies. The main difference between them—and it was an important one—was that the Soviet Union had abolished the traditional capitalist class, the stock-owning bourgeoisie, and replaced it with a collectivized layer of bureaucrats. Nazi Germany, and the other fascist countries, left the old capitalist class in place (except for the Jewish capitalists) and still owning property—although they now had to pay off the fascist rulers. This became clear at the end of the Second World War, when German and Italian capitalists re-emerged, still owning their firms and ready to carry on business.

State Capitalism and the Socialist Program

From the thirties to the eighties, there were sharp debates among Marxists about the nature of the Soviet Union (and later of its offspring). I find it astonishing how few sought to compare it to Engels's model of state capitalism. Many theorists insisted that the very concept of state capitalism contradicted Marxism—in spite of Marx and Engels's clear statements. What this means is that the condition that Marx and Engels saw as the culmination of capitalist decay, a great many Marxists see as the basic model of socialism.

For Engels, nationalization of all industry by a capitalist state was not socialism but what we today would call state (or statified) capitalism. Up to this point, anarchists agree with Engels and Marx. But Marx and Engels further believed that, if the workers were to take over the statified economy, with their *own* state, the result would be not state capitalism, but the beginning of socialism. For them, a collectivized economy would lead to the end of classes and the state, and the state would become a benign, noncoercive, institution. As Engels put it: "The proletariat seizes political power and turns the means of production in the first instance into state property. But in doing this, it abolishes itself as proletariat, abolishes all class distinctions and class antagonisms, abolishes also the state as state…. The government of persons is replaced by the administration of things, and by the conduct of processes of production. The state is not 'abolished.' It dies out" (1954, 388, 389).

As an anarchist, of course, I reject this perspective. As Kropotkin wrote in an article for the 1910 *Encyclopedia Britannica*, "The anarchists consider…that to hand over to the state all the main sources of economic life—the land, the mines, the railroads, banking, insurance, and so on— as also the management of all the main branches of industry, in addition to all the functions already accumulated in its hands (education, state-supported religions, defense of the territory, etc.) would mean to create a new instrument of tyranny. State capitalism would only increase the powers of bureaucracy and capitalism" (1975, 109–110). It makes no difference whether this involves a bourgeois state or a so-called workers' state.

With the benefit of over a century of hindsight, it is clear who was right. (For further discussion of state capitalism, see Daum 1990; Hobson and Tabor 1988; and Part III of Price 2010.)

Part III:

The Socialist Goal

Chapter 7: Socialism or Barbarism?

HOW would a proletarian revolution occur, in Marx's view? According to his "General Law of Capitalist Accumulation," there will be increasing economic, social, and political polarization. At the top is a small, concentrated layer of very rich people, served by salaried employees. There will be fewer but larger semi-monopolies, increasingly integrated with banks, speculators, and with the state. At the other economic pole are the workers, their wages and salaries under constant pressure. Below them are increasing layers of unemployed workers and a growing pool of the very poor, in the industrialized capitalist countries and worldwide in the poorest nations. There is increasing "entanglement of all peoples in the net of the world-market" (Marx 1906, 836).

The laws of capital, however distorted in practice, will not cease. In capitalism's epoch of decline, the rate of profit declines. Stagnation increases and whatever growth occurs is one-sided and unbalanced (development here, decline there). Unemployment, underemployment, underuse of productive capacity, economic crises, inflation and deflation, fictitious capital replacing accumulation of real capital, pools of poverty even in the richest nations, "underdevelopment" in the most oppressed nations. There are constant wars as well as ecological disasters: This pretty much sums up our world today, doesn't it?

Marx expected the working class to respond. He believed that the system itself pushes workers to become conscious of their situation and to rebel. "With the accumulation of capital," he said, "the class struggle, and, therefore, the class-consciousness of the working-men, develops" (717).

> [There] grows the revolt of the working class, a class always increasing in numbers, and disciplined, united, organized by the very mechanism of the process of capitalist production itself. The monopoly of capital becomes a fetter upon the mode of production, which has sprung up and flourished along with, and under it. Centralization of the means of production and socialization of labor at last reach a point where they become incompatible with their capitalist integument. This integument is burst asunder. The knell of capitalist private property sounds. The expropriators are expropriated…. Capitalist production begets, with the inexorability of a law of nature, its own negation…cooperation and the possession in common of the land and of the means of production. (836–837)

The Working Class?

Given Marx's general forecast, critics have raised various objections. One involves its focus on the rebellion of the working class (let alone of "working men"). Some critics point out that the working class has never made a successful socialist revolution (leaving aside the ambiguous case of Russia 1917). They add that the US working class, in particular, includes a great many people with conservative, even far-right, views, and the rest tend to be moderates or, at most, liberals.

This might suggest looking elsewhere for sources of rebellion, the critics argue. There are non-proletarian classes that are economically exploited (particularly the peasants; still a large class on a world scale, if not in North America). There are also non-class forms of oppression—of women, People of Color, oppressed nationalities, LGBT people, the physically disabled, and many more. And there are plenty of issues that might not seem, on the surface, directly related to class, with war and ecological decline topping the list. Revolutionary consciousness and outright revolt might certainly result from any of these, leading some to the conclusion that the workers' class struggle is only one of, say, three or five key struggles.

In practice, such political conclusions may not be very different from those of a sophisticated Marxist or class-struggle anarchist. However, other theorists have concluded that the struggle of the working class should be dismissed as unimportant because workers are supposedly even less likely to rebel than other oppressed sections of the population. This view definitely contradicts the core of Marx's Marxism, and rejects a key component of revolutionary, class-struggle, anarchist-communism. Still, many Marxists and anarchists agree with this rejection of working class struggle. Marxist-Leninists, for instance, pay lip service to the working class, but accept peasant-based armies led by Stalinist dictators, as in China, as socialist revolutions, and accept governments without worker control as "dictatorships of the proletariat."

Marx and Engels never claimed that the workers' socialist movement was the only struggle of interest. As a young man, before he became a communist, Marx had been a leader in the fight for bourgeois democracy, and he never stopped supporting all movements to expand democracy, such as the British Chartists, whether or not they were directly tied to the class struggle. After becoming a communist, he supported the national liberation of Poland and of Ireland, and joined the British labor movement's effort to support the North in the US Civil War, in alliance with the most extreme abolitionists. Mostly, though, Marx and Engels saw the need for the working class to ally itself with other oppressed and exploited groups in order to further their cause. At the end of his life, Engels was trying to persuade the German Social Democratic Party to develop a program with which to attract the mass of (mostly conservative) peasants. Of course, Marx and Engels never had an adequate understanding of all oppression—who does, even today?—but they were far from advocating a working-class-only perspective.

They did, however, put the working class at the heart of their strategy for liberating society. They thought that, at bottom, civilization was a system for the exploitation of working people. It was from surplus value that the rulers got their wealth. At the very least, this form of economic oppression overlapped with and interacted with all other forms of oppression. Should the workers, especially those at the very bottom of society, rise up, they would shake the system to its foundations, hopefully loosening the grip of every form of oppression. In the words of the *Communist Manifesto*,

> All previous movements were movements of minorities in the interest of minorities. The proletarian movement is the independent movement of the immense majority in the interest of the immense majority. The proletariat, the lowest stratum of present-day society, cannot raise itself up, cannot stand erect, without bursting asunder the whole superstructure of strata that make up official society.... The communist revolution is the most radical break with the traditional property relations; no wonder that in the course of its development there is the most radical break with traditional ideas." (1998, 133, 153)

It was not that the workers were more oppressed than anyone else, or that their oppression was more morally reprehensible. Marx's focus has more to do with strategy: Because they produce the wealth of society, workers have their hands on the means of production and distribution. They have the potential power to stop society in its tracks and even to start it up in a different way. And it is in their direct self-interest to do so. They are the ones immediately oppressed by capitalist exploitation; it is more likely that workers will rebel against exploitation than capitalists, shopkeepers, or police.

Because it includes anyone who must sell their labor power to live (or anyone who depends on those who must, such as their spouses or children), and who is not a supervisor, the modern working class is the vast majority of society. It also includes elements of every other section of society that is oppressed in every other way (women, African-Americans, immigrants, etc.). Workers' interests are not opposed to the rest of the oppressed.

Throughout history, proletarians have formed organizations that fought for a better world for themselves and others. This included large union federations as well as socialist or communist parties or anarchist federations. Repeatedly, they have rebelled, with everything from small strikes to actual revolutions. In over a century and a half, the modern working class has rebelled more often and more thoroughly than any other oppressed class in thousands of years.

Nonetheless, it is true that most workers in the United States are presently pro-capitalist. as are many workers in other countries. We do not seem on the verge of a revolution. If the working class majority is not ready for a socialist revolution, then there will not (yet) be a socialist revolution. But when they are ready…

Is Socialism Inevitable?

This brings up another set of questions about Marx's revolutionary perspective. Was he saying that the proletarian revolution *must* happen or only that it *could* happen? What did he mean when he wrote, "Capitalist production begets, with the inexorability of a law of nature, its own negation" (Marx 1906, 837)? The word "inexorability" seems to present the revolutionary process as an automatic process, like a chemical or biological "law of nature." Furthermore, Marx gets his concept of "negation" from Hegelian dialectics. Hegel presented history as a part of nature, moving automatically through the zigzags of the dialectic to its final but preordained goal. Employing a doctrine philosophers call "teleology," Hegel imagined that history had a built-in purpose—which just happened to be fulfilling his own philosophical system and, more concretely, the bureaucratic Prussian monarchy. In the end, neither science nor dialectics seem to leave much room for human consciousness and choice to affect history.

Marx seems to follow this logic. In the *Communist Manifesto*, he asserts, "What the bourgeoisie therefore produces, above all, are its own grave-diggers. Its fall and the victory of the proletariat are equally inevitable" (in Draper 1998, 135). This, of course, implies that history is an automatic mechanism, something that happens to people rather than something that people do. The most the working class can do is speed up the inevitable processes, but not to make them occur in the first place. This has been the main interpretation of Marxism among Social Democratic parties and Marxist-Leninists.

This inevitablism dovetails with what we might call Marx's "non-moral" approach. Nowhere in his work did he ever suggest that people *should* be for socialism, that it was morally right to fight for it, or that ethics were a necessary component for a vision of a good society. Supposedly, socialism would be a product of natural processes. As anyone who reads them knows, his writings—like his life—are filled with a moral passion, but it is not an acknowledged part of his theory.

The Italian anarchist Errico Malatesta complained that his admired mentor Peter Kropotkin had a somewhat similar orientation: unrealistically optimistic, mechanistic, and fatalist, not unlike the Marxists. "Since, according to his philosophy, that which occurs, must necessarily occur, so also the communist-anarchism he desired must inevitably triumph as if by a law of nature.... The bourgeois world was destined to crumble; it was already breaking up and revolutionary action only served to hasten the process" (Malatesta 1984, 265). Except that Kropotkin, unlike Marx, also believed in revolution as a moral cause, and sought to develop a naturalistic ethics.

The proletarian revolution and the preceding bourgeois revolution are different in an important way. Capitalism is an unplanned system. It works through the "invisible hand" of the market, through supply and demand and the law of value. As capitalist institutions gradually develop, the remaining feudal institutions stand in their way. Once the remnants of medievalism are wiped off the slate, the market will expand on its own. The bourgeoisie and their champions do not have to be fully aware of what they are doing. Conscious awareness seems, in general, a dangerous thing. The bourgeoisie, for instance, could never tell revolutionary peasants and artisans the truth: that the people's help was needed to overthrow the aristocracy, only to set up a new system of exploitation.

But libertarian-democratic communism is different. It is a society in which people deliberately and collectively regulate their economic interactions. The workers must make the revolution with full consciousness of what they are doing. The automatic laws of the market (the law of value) will only be overcome through workers' democracy, which means making conscious choices. This requires an understanding of how capitalism works (which Marx's economic theory mostly provides) but also requires a vision of an alternate society of freely associated, self-managed, producers (which Marx's economic theory mostly does not provide). Anything else leads in a state capitalist direction.

The inevitablist interpretation can have unfortunate political consequences. It can justify limiting struggle to reformism, since any struggle will (supposedly) inevitably lead to revolution. It can even justify a lack of struggle (Malatesta cites various anarchists who retired to private life, confident that the world would reach communist-anarchism without needing them to make any effort). It can lead to the Leninists' repression and mass murder, since they believed that they knew that it would come out all right in the end, in socialist freedom. Non-moralism and inevitablism became a problem when "history" produced something calling itself "socialist" that was actually a mass-murdering totalitarianism. Most revolutionary Marxists found themselves accepting such vile regimes as "actually existing socialism."

It can also lead in a conservative direction. If we interpret Marx as predicting that the working class will inevitably make a socialist revolution, then, since it has not, the whole theory must be mistaken and the program of socialist revolution must be rejected. Many have reasoned this way.

The Moral Choice

However, Marx and Engels sometimes used a different formulation. The beginning of the *Communist Manifesto* says, "The history of all hitherto existing society is the history of class struggles…. a fight that each time ended, either in a revolutionary re-constitution of society at large, or in the common ruin of the contending classes" (in Draper 1998, 105–107). Draper explains this as "either a revolution that remakes society or the collapse of the old order to a lower level" (200). Marx may have had the fate of ancient Rome in mind.

Engels restated this several times throughout his *Anti-Duhring*. He wrote that the bourgeoisie is "a class under whose leadership society is racing to ruin like a locomotive [with a] jammed safety-valve," and that the modern working class must make the socialist revolution or face "sinking to the level of a Chinese coolie." (1954, 217–218). For the capitalist class, "its own productive forces have grown beyond its control, and…are driving the whole of bourgeois society toward *ruin, or revolution*" (228; my emphasis). When the capitalist system turns most people into proletarians, "it creates the power which, *under penalty of its own destruction,* is forced to accomplish this revolution" (388; my emphasis).

Socialist revolution is not inevitable. Engels is presenting it as a possible choice. If, in this epoch of capitalist decay, we do not choose it, our society faces destruction (in fact, he predicted World War I). The working class could be reduced to the level of the starving, super-exploited,

Chinese workers of that time. Therefore, the working class and its allies should consciously and deliberately decide to make the revolution (as we, the revolutionary minority, want it to).

Engels did not specifically call this a moral choice. For him, it remains implicit: There is very little ethical reasoning involved in preferring socialist revolution to the ruin of the working class and all society. Although many of us regard it as a weakness that ethical issues are not front and center, the main issue for Engels is whether we agree with the political-economic analysis.

Where Engels said the alternatives were "ruin or revolution," the revolutionary-democratic, Marxist, Rosa Luxemburg, saw them as "socialism or barbarism" (Geras 1976). She believed capitalism was in its final epoch, propping itself up through imperialism, which would lead to greater crises and devastating world wars. She foresaw that capitalism, if unhindered, would destroy cultures and populations, would create deserts where there had been cities and nations. She was accused of believing that the economic collapse of capitalism was inevitable. What she believed was that *if capitalism was left alone* to follow out its own dynamic laws of development, it would eventually collapse, and produce "barbarism." This was "inevitable." But she argued, if the working class chooses to intervene in history, it will be able to prevent barbarism and collapse; it will be able to save humanity by making a socialist revolution.

The anarchist Murray Bookchin noted that the hierarchical structures of modern capitalism threaten human survival through nuclear war or ecological catastrophe (he wrote before global warming became so obvious). "No longer are we faced with Marx's famous choice of socialism or barbarism; we are confronted with the more drastic alternatives of anarchism or annihilation. The problems of necessity and survival have become congruent with the problems of freedom and life" (1986, 62).

In its epoch of decay, capitalism threatens humanity with terrible destruction. That is why a revolution is necessary. If this were not so, then socialism (of some sort) might be a nice ideal, a morally attractive goal, but little else. There would be no need to ask workers and others to engage in great struggles, to risk everything in a revolution, if capitalist society might continue on a course of gradual improvement, with ups and downs in the economy. Indeed, *it would be wrong to advocate a revolution*, with all its uncertainties, and its costs in resources and blood.

Ironically, while threatening global destruction, capitalist industrialism has also made a new, nonoppressive, classless society possible. Its technology is so immensely productive that it could provide plenty for everyone, with only a minimum of labor and plenty of leisure time. The technology would have to be redesigned to fit a sustainable ecology and a self-managed economy, but the potential is there.

Will the working class take up the challenge? Major aspects of capitalism push them toward class consciousness and revolution. But there are contradictory, conservatizing aspects that hold them back. Some workers are (relatively) better off than the majority of the world's workers (in the United States this includes many white, unionized, skilled, and/or white-collar workers). Marx and Engels sometimes called this layer of proletarians, the "labor aristocracy." These workers may be bought off, corrupted, or simply satisfied with the way things are. At the opposite pole is a mass of very poor workers, including the super-exploited (paid less than society's standard for their labor-power commodity) and the unemployed. They may be exhausted, demoralized, and overwhelmed, feeling uninterested in economic or political struggle. While Marx believed that the class-consciousness-creating aspects of capitalism would eventually win out, really there can be no guarantee that either layer of the working class, or any other, will engage in struggle at any particular time or place.

Marx believed that socialism was only possible when technology had become potentially productive enough. Only this allowed a return to the equality and freedom of early human hunter-gatherer societies but with a much higher standard of living. In the past, socialism (communism) was simply not possible. (Hunter-gatherer societies had "primitive communism" in the sense that no one "owned" the land or the flora and fauna. But societies lived through cycles of plenty and of starvation.) There was not enough to go around. After previous revolutions, most people had to go back to the daily grind in order to keep everyone fed, while a few rulers were able to live off that labor. Successful mass struggles might produce more freedom, but they could not jump from a low level of productivity to socialist liberation.

But productivity has greatly expanded. For example, until quite recently in human history, 95 percent of the population raised food, so that 5 percent or less could live in cities and have an urban culture. Today, in the industrialized nations, the proportions are reversed. Less than 5 percent of the population produces more than enough food to feed the rest of the nation. Even if we switched to fully organic methods of farming, the proportion of those who have to do farm work would be much smaller than they have been for most of history. A society that satisfies the needs and wants of all its members is possible, under socialism.

Kropotkin noted that, in the past,

> The power of production of food-stuffs and of all industrial commodities had not yet reached the perfection they have attained now. In those times communism was truly considered as equivalent to general poverty and misery, and well-being was looked at as something which is accessible to a very small number only. But this quite real and extremely important obstacle to communism exists no more. Owing to the immense productivity of human labor…a very high degree of well-being can easily be obtained in a few years by communist work." (2002, 172)

Marx and Kropotkin could neither prove nor disprove this assessment (without access to an alternate universe). If they were wrong, if it was possible to achieve socialism at any time since people began agriculture ten thousand years ago, then humans have been failing to create socialism for ten thousand years. This does not make our future chances look good. But if socialist freedom has only been possible for a century or two at most, due to the development of the necessary "immense productivity of human labor," then we've been missing our opportunity for only a short time, historically speaking. It suggests that we still have a chance to create a free and cooperative society—before catastrophe overtakes us.

In 1858, Marx wrote to Engels, "The difficult question for us is this. On the continent, the revolution is imminent and will immediately assume a socialist form. But will it not necessarily be crushed in this small corner of the earth, seeing that over a far greater area the movement of bourgeois society is still in the ascendant?" (in Buber 1958, 84–85). Marx was an internationalist, and here he was expressing a realistic fear that the European socialist revolution would be held back by the lack of economic development on a world scale. And so it was. Marx did not realize that capitalism was not yet in its final epoch but only reaching the height of its development. Today industrial capitalism has entered its epoch of decline. Humanity has reached and passed the point where it is capable of industrializing the whole world.

Despite humanity's powerful modern technology, a great deal would have to be done to redevelop the world under socialism. The "underdeveloped" (misdeveloped) oppressed parts of the world would have to be industrialized, according to their wishes and wants, in an ecological way. The former imperialist parts of the world would have to be re-industrialized in a way that is ecologically sustainable, no longer destroying the natural environment. Production everywhere would have to be reconfigured to make it democratic, without order-givers and order-takers. The destruction created by any revolutionary vs. counterrevolutionary civil wars would have to be repaired. Meanwhile (economically wasteful) armaments would still be produced so long as capitalist states still threaten the socialist regions. All this can be done, on the way to the full achievement of libertarian communism.

The alternatives, then, are *"a revolutionary re-constitution of society at large or the common ruin of the contending classes"* (Marx), *"ruin or revolution"* (Engels), *"socialism or barbarism"* (Luxemburg), *"anarchism or annihilation"* (Bookchin). With this interpretation, Marx and others declared that what capitalism produces, "with the inexorability of a law of nature," is the end of capitalist prosperity and stability, one way or another. The good times, such as they were, could not last. The still-open question is what will replace it.

It may still seem deterministic and teleological to say that we will face one of two possible futures. However, both "a revolutionary re-constitution of society" and "common ruin" could take many possible forms. The "re-constitution" might involve various methods of revolution leading to various forms of socialism (see the Appendix). "Common ruin" could mean various forms of destruction, including wars, economic degradation, and/or a range of ecological disasters.

As best as we can predict, capitalism inevitably creates the possibility of an alternate society, built by the working class and its socialized labor. Its situation in life pushes the working class to struggle against its oppression. This tends to create a consciousness of exploitation and a desire for a new society. The beautiful vision of socialism, the culmination of the moral values of humanity down through the ages, has become a real possibility and even a necessity.

But it is still a choice. It is not inevitable at all that workers, or anyone else, will chose revolution before we face economic collapse, nuclear war, or environmental cataclysm. It is only possible. It is less a matter of prediction than commitment. Whatever is the "correct" interpretation of Marx on the question of inevitability, the issue will be decided in struggle.

Chapter 8: What Marx Meant by Socialism and Communism

THE "utopian" socialists who preceded Marx, such as Charles Fourier, Robert Owen, and Étienne Cabet, created very detailed instructions on how a new society should be organized. Marx deliberately rejected that approach. His descriptions of how a socialist or communist economy would work are few and far between. (Marx referred to his goal as both "socialism" and "communism," although he preferred the latter; the same is true of most revolutionary anarchists—though the term's association with Communist dictatorships has made it less attractive). He developed a critique of capitalism, not of socialism, and what he wrote about the latter tended to be limited. In volume one of *Capital*, for instance, Marx refers to "a community of free individuals, carrying on their work with the means of production in common, in which the labor-power of all the different individuals is consciously applied as the combined labor-power of the community"(90). Their work would be "consciously regulated by them in accordance with a settled plan" (92).

Rather than presenting a new social system, Marx focused on the need for the working class to collectively take power, to replace the bourgeoisie as the (temporarily) new ruling class. The workers and their allies would get rid of the existing state and replace it with a radically democratic state, similar to the Paris Commune. This new state would essentially be the self-organized working class, and it would expropriate the capitalist class, allowing workers to build a new economy based on the centralization, collectivization, and socialization of labor of the existing monopolized and statified capitalist economy. The means of production (but not individual consumer goods) would be held in common. An economic plan would be agreed upon (although he never spelled out how).

In a truly socialist economy, there would be no more law of value, because goods would not be bought and sold on the market. There will be no commodities. Workers would distribute their labor among various industries according to need, as determined by whatever plan they had created. Established through revolution, Marx maintained, the workers' state as a coercive social machine would "wither away" or "die out." It would evolve into a nonviolent public institution coordinating the economy. Classes as distinct layers of society, specialized to either be workers or bosses, would also dissolve into a classless society. Labor would be unalienated because it would not be done for someone else. It would be done for the community of which each person was a free member. The social nature of all interactions would be transparent rather than fetishized, clear to everyone. The very nature of work would change, ending class-determined divisions of labor and unequal relations between town and countryside.

Transitional Program of the *Communist Manifesto*

Section II of the 1848 *Communist Manifesto* is titled, "Proletarians and Communists." At its end, Marx lays out a brief program. It is not a description of full communism, but a series of steps toward communism, a transitional program. First, he writes, the working class must take power. Then, "the proletariat will use its political supremacy to wrest, by degrees, all capital from the bourgeoisie, to centralize all instruments of production in the hands of the state, i.e., of the proletariat organized as the ruling class...by means of despotic inroads on the rights of property..." (in Draper 1998, 155). He follows this with a ten-point program that includes, "5. Centralization of credit in the hands of the state... 6. Centralization of the means of communication and transport in the hands of the state. 7. Extension of factories and instruments of production owned by the state.... 8. Equal liability of all to labor. Establishment of industrial armies, especially for agriculture" (ibid).

This would lead to the end of distinct, specialized classes, Marx claimed. It would also lead to the end of the state, that is, the end of a coercive instrument of one class over other classes. "When, in the course of development... all production has been concentrated in the hands of associated individuals, the public power loses its political character.... In place of the old bourgeois society with its classes and class antagonisms there comes an association in which the free development of each is the precondition for the free development of all" (157). Anarchists, of

course, doubt the chances of such free individual development if the "public power" has all industry and agriculture
centralized into its control and everyone is forced to ("has
liability to") work in industrial armies.

By 1872, even Marx and Engels themselves felt that "this
program has in some details become antiquated." They did
not go into much detail, but wrote in their Preface to that
year's German edition of *The Communist Manifesto*, "One
thing especially was proved by the [Paris] Commune, viz.,
that 'the working class cannot simply lay hold of the ready
made state machinery and wield it for its own purposes'"
(262). They were actually quoting Marx's *The Civil War in
France* here (Marx and Engels 1971, 68). In that essay, Marx
claimed it was not enough to radically democratize the
bourgeois state. Instead, it was necessary to completely get
rid of the capitalist state and replace it with an institution
like the Paris Commune. "The centralized state power," he
wrote "with its ubiquitous organs of standing army, police, bureaucracy, clergy, and judicature—organs wrought
after the plan of a systematic and hierarchic division of
labor—originates from the days of absolute monarchy"
(ibid). While the emerging bourgeoisie used elements of
the monarchial state as a weapon against feudalism, they
also gradually changed it into something better suited to
their needs. Governance was "placed under parliamentary
control—that is, under the direct control of the propertied
classes" (69), which allowed different factions of the ruling
class a forum in which to work out their differences. But
whatever those differences, the bourgeois state remained a
repressive force when it came to the workers: "At the same

pace at which the progress of modern industry developed, widened, intensified the class antagonism between capital and labor, the state power assumed more and more the character of the national power of capital over labor, of a public force organized for social enslavement, of an engine of class despotism" (69). The idea of "wielding" this sort of institution for revolutionary ends made little sense. But what would replace it?

In Marx and Engels' writings, they portray the 1871 Paris Commune uprising as extremely democratic. In particular, they noted, the city council members were directly elected by the sections (neighborhoods) of the city and were subject to recall if their sections no longer agreed with them. The representatives were paid as much as average workers. All officials, such as judges and local police, were similarly elected and controllable. The regular army was replaced by an armed people (a volunteer militia). Marx expected that if the Commune had lasted it would have federated with similar city, town, and village communes throughout France.

This was an image of a very democratic representative democracy. But it contained nothing of direct democracy, of the members of sections meeting and deciding how to manage their neighborhood. Or of workers meeting face-to-face in the factory or shop or office each morning to decide what they would do that day in accordance with their overall plan. In general, anarchists are not against some degree of representation or delegation, in large, complex societies. But anarchists seek to root this in a vibrant, lively, decentralized, direct democracy, where communities directly control their lives. Even at their most libertarian-democratic, Marx and Engels showed no understanding of this.

Critique of the Gotha Program

In *The Critique of the Gotha Program,* Marx described communism as a "cooperative society based on common ownership of the means of production" (1992, 345). He raised the notion of two "phases" of communism. In the first phase, we are dealing with "a communist society, not as it has *developed* on its own foundations, but, on the contrary, just as it *emerges* from capitalist society. In every respect, economically, morally, and intellectually, it is thus still stamped with the birthmarks of the old society from whose womb it emerges" (346).

For some reason, Lenin renamed Marx's "first phase of communist society" *socialism* and only called Marx's "more advanced phase of communist society" *communism* proper. To Marx, they were both phases of communism. (And neither has any relation to the later differences between Socialist and Communist parties.)

Of all the possible differences between the lower and higher phase of communism, Marx focused on the issue of remuneration of the workers, which was a highly contentious issue at the time. (He presented his views as a prediction, rather than as the proposal they really were.) In the first phase, he expected that individual workers would receive payment equal to the amount of work they contributed (minus deductions for an overall fund for maintenance and accumulation of production capacity, and for taking care of children, the sick, and older people). The able-bodied workers would be—Marx predicted—paid in certificates that register how many hours they worked or how hard (duration or intensity of labor); they would not to be rewarded according to how much they produced. Marx did not propose that more skilled or highly trained workers be paid at a higher rate. The certificates would not be money; they could not be accumulated or exchanged for goods on a market. Instead, they are brought to the common storehouse to exchange for goods that took an equivalent amount of labor to produce: Ten hours of work earned the right to a shirt that took an average of ten hours to make. Only consumer goods could be withdrawn, not means of production.

To Marx, this was better than capitalism but still limited. It was only the first phase of communism. Receiving goods equivalent to labor performed is still "in principle a bourgeois right," although one which capitalism had never lived up to. Workers differ in strength and ability—some can work longer or harder than others. Workers also have different needs and wants, regardless of how hard they work. Therefore this remunerative "equality" remains unequal and unfair. The society, it implies, is not yet completely unalienated.

In an advanced communist society, however, "when labor is no longer just a means of keeping alive but has itself become a vital need; when the all-round development of individuals has also increased their productive powers and all the springs of cooperative wealth flow more abundantly—only then can society wholly cross the narrow horizon of bourgeois right and inscribe on its banner: From each according to his abilities, to each according to his needs!" (347).

And what of the political realm, Marx asks? "In a communist society…what social functions will remain that are analogous to the present functions of the state?" (355). While he did not directly answer the question, he suggested that there may still be a need for social coordination and other tasks in a stateless society, adding that, "Between capitalist and communist society lies a period of revolutionary transformation from one to the other. There is a corresponding period of transition in the political sphere and in this period the state can only take the form of a revolutionary dictatorship of the proletariat" (355).

What exactly Marx and Engels meant by the "revolutionary dictatorship of the proletariat" is a matter of controversy (see Draper 1986, 1987; Price 2007). With the development of Marxism-Leninism it came to mean the dictatorship of one political party or a small group—or even one person. Marx's belief that there would be a transitional period between capitalism and communism, as well as his division of communism itself into lower and higher phases, have been used as an excuse for Stalinist totalitarianism. It has been used to justify regimes that were not moving toward stateless, classless associations of free individuals—but that were, in fact, moving in the other direction.

None of these rationalizations would have been acceptable to Marx or Engels's democratic principles. In their day, "dictatorship" could refer to domination by a parliament or by a popular class. As we can best determine, what they meant by "dictatorship of the proletariat," was neither more nor less than "the rule of the working class" (in the same sense that a bourgeois democracy would be called a "dictatorship of the bourgeoisie"). They pointed to the ultra-democratic Paris Commune as an example of the dictatorship of the proletariat. Some libertarian Marxists have used the term to mean the stateless rule of the self-organized working class. Lenin, in *State and Revolution* (written before he set up his own one-party dictatorship), claimed that Marx and Engels had meant a "semi-state" that, from the moment of its creation, would "immediately" begin to wither away as popular participation increased. Today, we should avoid using the phrase, given what it has come to mean to most people.

It is unclear whether Marx thought that the "period of revolutionary transformation…in the political sphere" would take place before the lower phase of communism or if the lower phase is part of that transformation. Presumably, the working class must first seize power before it can begin to create even the lower phase. (Keep in mind that, for anarchists, "seizing power" is not necessarily the same as "seizing state power." Overthrowing the bourgeois state and replacing it with a commune of workers' councils and popular assemblies—the self-organization of the workers and all oppressed—is quite different from creating a new bureaucratic-military state machine.)

This has become an issue relevant to the poorer, oppressed, nations of the world. As in Marx's day, most of the countries of the world have economies so warped by capitalism that even achieving a "lower" phase of communism would be a monumental task. They have severe poverty along with ecological destruction, and a productive economic sector mostly geared to export and enriching foreign imperialists and local bloodsuckers. But, unlike Marx's day, the world as a whole has more than enough resources (natural, technological, etc.) to establish a prosperous international communism.

What then are the options for an oppressed nation in Africa, Asia, or Latin America? Even if the workers, peasants, and other oppressed sections of the population seize power and set up their own federation of workers' and peasants' councils, what can they achieve? The federation would take steps toward communism, but these will be limited internally. Markets and the law of value can not be immediately abolished (as mentioned, Marx did not think that all aspects of capitalism could be immediately abolished, even in the lower stage of communism). The federation would work to spread the revolution to other oppressed nations and to the imperialist nations. The latter have the wealth to help the poor countries develop in their own way, toward liberatory communism. This is the strategy of the Permanent Revolution, applied internationally.

Some Marxists—Maoists, for instance—see revolution as a two-stage process: first a capitalist revolution to build a strong economic foundation, then the proletarian revolution. This is a distortion of Marx's views. Workers and their allies should not be limited to the program of capitalism and bourgeois-democracy. Marx and Engels believed that, whenever possible, the working class should lead all oppressed people to take power and carry out tasks of both the bourgeois-democratic revolution and the proletarian-socialist revolution. The first program includes land to the peasants who use it, freedom of speech, election of officials, national self-determination, etc., and the second program includes also public ownership of the land and industry, worker management and planning of industry, international revolution, etc. These programs conflict in certain ways; for example, "land to the peasants" implies distributing large estates to landless peasants, which is not the eventual socialist goal of democratic collectivism. However, Marx and Engels believed that the peasants should be supported in their democratic demands and respectfully won over to socialism (including by sponsoring cooperatives). Similarly, each country and region would have to combine bourgeois-democratic and proletarian-democratic demands according to their own circumstances.

A Technological Revolution

Lenin appears to have interpreted Marxism to mean that modern technology and social organization, just as it is arranged under monopoly capitalism, will continue under socialism. The only difference would be that, on top, instead of corporate boards of directors and the bourgeois state, there will be a centralized workers' state. But Marx and Engels understood that much of technology was developed for no reason but to increase the exploitation of the workers.

Society cannot free itself unless every individual is freed. The old mode of production must therefore be revolutionized from top to bottom, and in particular the former division of labor must disappear. Its place must be taken by an organization of production in which…productive labor, instead of being a means of subjugating men, will become a means of their emancipation, by offering each individual the opportunity to develop all his faculties, physical and mental, in all directions and exercise them to the full—in which, therefore, productive labor will become a pleasure instead of being a burden. (Engels 1954, 408)

For Marx, the "more advanced phase of communist society" begins once "the enslaving subjugation of individuals to the division of labor and thereby the antithesis of intellectual and physical labor" is over (1992, 347). The most alienating division of labor, then, was between intellectual and physical labor, between making decisions and carrying them out, between order-giving and order-taking. The "utopians" had developed the idea of integrating labor, and the anarchists were to develop it further, but it was also important to Marx and Engels. It was a technical integration that included the synthesis of agriculture with manufacturing industries: "gradual abolition of the distinction between town and country, by a more equable distribution of population over the country…" (Marx and Engels 1998, 155). This was social but also necessary for ecological reasons: "The present poisoning of the air, water and land can be put an end to only by the fusion of town and country" (1954, 411). But Engels also considered the idea of collective townships integrating agriculture and industry to be utopian without a centralized plan: "Only a society which makes it possible for its productive forces to dovetail harmoniously into each other on the basis of one single vast plan can allow industry to be distributed over the whole country" (411).

Comparisons of Marx's Communism and Anarchist Communism

Marx and Engels deliberately did not give details about what a socialist/communist society would look like. We can, however, get some ideas from what they wrote. They were committed to a democratic society, self-managed by freely associated producers. They saw it as being a centrally planned economy (with "a single vast plan"). Industry and agriculture would be integrated, and owned by the democratic workers' state that had replaced the bourgeois state. The workers' state would begin to disintegrate as soon as it was established, due to increasing participation of the working people in the coordination and planning of their lives, as well as an increase in unalienated labor.

Presumably the society Marx and Engels imagined would still be centralized. That is where problems arise. Centralization is more than unification or coordination. It means that there is a center and a periphery. Even if the center's officials are popularly elected, the center is managed by a few people who get information from the many at the periphery, who in turn carry out the directions given them from the center.

Here, Marx and Engels can be contrasted with Peter Kropotkin. His anarchist vision was of a pluralistic and decentralized federalism. Kropotkin also did not draw up a detailed program, but he discussed in several books how free working people might reorganize a city and its region after a revolution (e.g., *Fields, Factories, and Workshops* and *The Conquest of Bread)*. He wrote that voluntary associations would

> substitute themselves for the state in all its functions. They would represent an interwoven network, composed of an infinite variety of groups and federations of all sizes and degrees, local, regional, national, and international—temporary or more or less permanent—for all possible purposes: production, consumption, and exchange, communications, sanitary arrangements, education, mutual protection, defense of the territory, and so on; and, on the other side, for the satisfaction of an ever-increasing number of scientific, artistic, literary and sociable needs.... True progress lies in the direction of decentralization, both territorial and functional, in the development of the spirit of local and personal initiative, and of free federation from the simple to the compound, in lieu of the present hierarchy from the center to the periphery. (2002, 284, 286)

Kropotkin did not believe in a workers' state, an institution that supposedly represented the working class but that—as a state—was separated from and above it. As seen in the quote above, he proposed federated associations for "mutual protection [and] defense of the territory," tasks that, while necessary, did not require a state. He also rejected the concept of two phases of communism. He thought that a revolution should be immediately followed by full communism, but that able-bodied adults would be expected to work a half-day, perhaps five hours, to earn a guaranteed minimum of food, clothing, and shelter. They would then be free to do voluntary work for luxuries. (For further discussion of an anarchist approach to a post-capitalist, post-revolutionary economy, see the Appendix to Chapter 8: Malatesta's Method for an Anarchist Economy.)

Anarchist and Marxist visions are not absolute alternatives. Kropotkin's federated associations could democratically work out an overall economic plan. On the other hand, in *The Civil War in France,* Marx, for once, described a non-state vision of self-governing industries (he was making a point, not advocating a program). He remarked that there are bourgeois ideologists who declare that communism is "impossible," but who also advocate producer (worker-managed) cooperatives. Sounding almost like an anarcho-syndicalist, Marx responded that the Paris Commune,

> intended to abolish that class property which makes the labor of the many the wealth of the few. It aimed at the expropriation of the expropriators. It wanted to make individual property a truth by transforming the means of production, land, and capital, now

chiefly the means of enslaving and exploiting labor, into mere instruments of free and associated labor. But this is communism, "impossible" communism!... If co-operative production is not to remain a sham and a snare; if it is to supersede the capitalist system; if united co-operative societies are to regulate national production upon common plan, thus taking it under their own control... what else, gentlemen, would it be but communism, "possible" communism? (1971, 75–76)

What else indeed?

Conclusion: An Anarchist Critique of Marx's Political Economy

MARX'S economic theory is distinctive in several ways. He started from the issue of how labor is used and organized to produce and distribute goods and services. In order to consume things, people have to work to produce and distribute them, and they have to organize their labor to do so. This focus on the process of labor makes it possible to see how modern workers are exploited like the serfs and slaves before them. Some work and others live off that work (even if they spend some effort in organizing those who work and in making sure that they do not rebel). Alternate theories obfuscate this reality.

Marx saw capitalism as a dynamic *historical* system, driven by internal conflicts. It had an origin; it reached its height; it began to decline; and it will end. In this it is no different from previous socio-economic systems (and if humanity makes it to libertarian communism, that too will evolve, although how is beyond our ability to predict). Bourgeois economists, however, write as if the categories of capitalism have applied for all time, or at least as if they expect the "free market" to go on forever, the perfect economic system, the "end of history."

Broadly speaking, Marx's analysis has held up well. Unlike the classical political economists, he predicted the continuation of the business cycle, with its conclusions in crises. Similarly, he predicted the growth of ever-larger capitalist enterprises, into semi-monopolies. He expected capitalism to have class conflicts, an ever-expanding world market, wars, and ecological decay.

Marx's critique of political economy provides a set of useful theoretical tools for understanding the present conditions of the capitalist economy and its likely future development. But the tools are no better than their user. As the old joke goes, Marxist economists have predicted ten of the last three recessions. More to the point, few Marxists predicted that World War II would be followed by an extended period of prosperity. Neither did many liberal or conservative economists, but Marxism was supposed to be superior. Once the post-war prosperity had settled in, most influential Marxist theorists declared that the epoch of capitalist decay was no longer in effect. Like almost all bourgeois economists, they said that the prosperity would last—and gave up revolutionary politics.

Most Marxist economists also did not apply Marx and Engels's concept of state capitalism to the Soviet Union or Maoist China. They supported these regimes; and the few who had not did not expect them to transform into traditional capitalism. Even now, few have much of an explanation for how this happened.

To be fair, understanding social structures (which is to say, people acting, thinking, and feeling, together) is difficult. Marx was trying to be as scientific in the social field as the hard, natural sciences, but this is probably impossible. For over thirty years, a few of us have been predicting the final collapse of the post-war prosperity, based on our understanding of Marxist political economy. Instead, the world economy has continued to gradually slide downhill, with ups and downs. I believe, with others, that 2008 was the beginning of a new period of crisis-ridden decline (see this book's reference section for further analyses).

Making such predictions, I often feel like a geologist in California saying, "Do not continue to build houses here; at some point there will be an enormous earthquake that will flatten cities." People ask this geologist, "When will this great earthquake occur?" The geologist does not know. "Maybe this year. Maybe in a decade or two. Possibly in a century." The response: "Forget about it! We will take our chances building our houses." Political economics is much more complex than geology. Unlike geological strata, classes and social groups have consciousness and make choices (people have "free will"). So it is hard to make predictions and harder to persuade people when we do.

The Problem with Marxism

Marxism came out of the same socialist and working class movements as anarchism did, and it shares many of the same values and goals. Its critique of political economy is valuable for understanding the economy and fighting capitalism. Yet Marxism's history, as a movement, has been gruesome. The Social-Democratic parties, directly influenced by Marx and Engels, became reformist, statist, counterrevolutionary, and pro-imperialist. They supported their warring imperialist states in World War I and fought against the Russian and German revolutions afterwards. They failed to fight the rise of fascism. In the Cold War, they supported Western imperialism and abandoned all claims to be for a new type of society. Lenin, Trotsky, and others tried to revive revolutionary Marxism during World War I and the Russian revolution. Instead, they established a one-party police state. Under Stalin, this evolved into several totalitarian state capitalisms that murdered tens of millions of workers and peasants around the world.

Marxism was not supposed to be a religious faith but a materialist praxis. As Engels liked to say, "The proof of the pudding is in the eating." How did something that seemed to have such good goals, good values, and good theory repeatedly end up so badly? What does that tell us about the theory?

Anarchism has certainly had its failures. It has done no better than Marxism in leading workers to socialist revolution. There were racist and authoritarian aspects to the views of Proudhon and Bakunin. Kropotkin violated anarchist principles by supporting the Allied imperialists in World War I. In the Spanish revolution of 1936–39, the mainstream anarchists abandoned their program and betrayed the working class by joining the liberal bourgeois government. They held back the workers' revolution, resulting in the victory of Spanish fascism. In Asia, Korean and Chinese anarchists gave support to the reactionary nationalist Chinese Kuomintang. Anarchist theory and practice has plenty of room for improvement—and I hope this book helps—but at least anarchists did not murder tens of millions of working people in the name of communism.

Throughout this work, I have referred to problems with Marx's theory. One is his centralism. His vision of socialism in certain ways seems to be a purified capitalism. It would build on the collectivization and socialization of labor that are created by capitalist monopolization and statification. These would be pulled together into a centralized agency (presumably run by a minority) that would develop a vast overall plan covering the whole economy. For all his writing about "freely associated individuals," he never considered the possibility of a decentralized, bottom-up form of democratic *economic* planning. At most he advocated an improved representative democracy, at work and in the community. But he never conceived of rooting it in face-to-face direct democracy.

Marx's problem was not crude statism as such. He did not worship the state or advocate totalitarianism. But he was influenced by the Jacobin tradition in European leftism. The state seemed to him to be the natural institution to integrate the whole economy, as it tended to do even under capitalism. Therefore, it made sense to use it (or to create a new state), which would then evolve into a non-state, noncoercive public structure. This view was tied to the main tactical difference between Marx and the anarchists in the First International, namely that he wanted it to sponsor workers' parties throughout Europe, to run for government offices, and they opposed this. I think that Marx's pro-centralization, pro-state, view played a major role in the post-Marx Marxists developing authoritarian visions of socialism and authoritarian politics in general.

Another main factor in the degeneration of post-Marx Marxism was somewhat more philosophical and subtle. It was the concept of capitalism moving "inevitably" and "inexorably" to socialism. The wheels grind on, the workers develop class consciousness sort of as a by-product, capitalism moves into crisis, and the workers revolt, creating the lower phase of communism (see Tabor 2004). As we've seen, this automatism is tied to Marx's non-moralism, his failure to connect the Marxist economic critique to any sort of ideal values (unlike the anarchist analyses of Proudhon, Bakunin, and Kropotkin). As he saw it, the workers will fight for socialism because the workers will fight for socialism, not because it is the morally right thing to do. Therefore there is no need to say much about what a socialist society would look like, as a goal to aim for, because it can be relied on to happen, to work itself out. As I have pointed out, there are sources within Marx and Engels's work that suggests that there are not one but (at least) two possibilities, which required a moral choice. But this was not emphasized by Marx or Engels and was easy to miss. Similarly, by scouring their writings, it is possible to find elements of a vision of a liberated communist society, one without a mental-manual division of labor, ecologically balanced, without a state, etc. But this also was rarely raised.

So what happens when history produces a totalitarian mass-murdering, state-capitalist nightmare that calls itself "socialist"? Most revolutionary Marxists decided that, since this was what came out of the historical process, it must be "actually existing socialism." So it had to be accepted. The idea of comparing it to a vision of a free association of cooperating individuals did not come up; for most Marxists, there was no such vision.

Marx presented his thinking as an integral whole. "Marxism" (or "scientific socialism") included the critique of political economy (my topic here). It included a broader background method for studying society: historical materialism. It included a philosophical approach: dialectical materialism. It included practical political strategies: building workers' electoral parties and labor unions.

This was a total worldview, justified because it was going to be the worldview of a rising new class, the proletariat. Because I cannot accept the totality of this worldview, I do not regard myself as a Marxist. I am a "Marxist-informed anarchist." The bourgeoisie, the current ruling class, has always had more than one philosophy, economic theory, and political strategy. Why not the working class?

As it turned out, Marxism, or something calling itself "Marxism," did become the ideology of a rising new class: the state-capitalist collective bureaucracy. Within the growing managerial and bureaucratic layer of capitalism, a section became radicalized, rejecting rule by the traditional bourgeoisie. Instead, they saw themselves as the new (benevolent) rulers. For them, a variety of Marxism became a justifying ideology and a guide to power. In the "Communist" countries, Marxism became a rationalization for keeping power. This development had been predicted by Bakunin and Kropotkin.

I do not at all deny the sincerity of Marx and Engels's libertarian-democratic, humanistic, and proletarian views. This was—and remains—a real and valuable aspect of Marx and Engels's Marxism, subjectively the heart of what they were trying to accomplish. But throughout history, class society has corrupted movements for liberation, turning them into tools of elites striving to replace the old rulers with themselves, using the people as a battering ram against the old order. Given the low level of productivity, it had to be so. There could not yet be a society of plenty for all and leisure for all. But now it is possible to win real human liberation. There is a technology that could help provide for *everyone's* needs—but that is threatened with total destruction, if not taken out of the hands of the ruling class. An international, socialized, working class is capable—potentially—of really achieving an unalienated society.

But the old pressures are still there. Whatever makes a movement vulnerable to becoming elitist, authoritarian, and undemocratic, weakens the revolutionary libertarian aspects of the movement. So it has proved with Marxism, despite its contributions. Then even the genuinely liberatory aspects of the theory, including its scientific critique of political economy, can be misused by the new elite. Bureaucrats have used even the truly democratic-libertarian aspects of Marxism to cover up the reality of state-capitalist tyranny. "Marxism" can serve as a distraction and a rationalization.

Libertarian Marxism

Writing of what I call the two sides of Marx's theory, the anarchist McKay claims "There are many continuities from Marx to Lenin, but there are also continuities from Marx to more libertarian Marxists...whose ideas approximate anarchism's desire for the free association of equals" (2008, 24). A range of people who accept Marx's views are anti-statist and close to anarchism in several ways. Known as libertarian Marxists, autonomist Marxists, left communists, or libertarian communists, they are distinct from both Leninism and social democracy.

For example, Paul Mattick expressed his anti-statist, council communist perspective this way:

> There is no room for a "socialist state" in socialism, even though there is the need for a central direction of the socialized economy, which, however, is itself a part of the organization of the associated producers and not an independent entity set against them.... It is not through the state that socialism can be realized, as this would exclude the self-determination of the working class, which is the essence of socialism. State rule perpetuates the divorce of the workers from the means of production...and thus also perpetuates class relations." (1983, 160–161)

Harry Cleaver (2000) claims to have first coined the phrase "autonomous Marxism." In this category he includes the "Johnson-Forest Tendency" of C.L.R. James,

Raya Dunayevskaya, and Grace Lee (Boggs); the Italian "workerists" from the "extraparliamentary" left, such as Antonio Negri, Mariarosa Dalla Costa, Mario Tronti, and others; and the British Marxist "bottom-up" historians such as E. P. Thompson and Christopher Hill (he does not mention the legacy of William Morris, but Thompson wrote a major book about him). He refers to Rosa Luxemburg, as well as council communists such as Anton Pannekoek and Paul Mattick. Interestingly, he says he learned from "anarcho-communists like Emma Goldman and Peter Kropotkin," even though they were not Marxists (14). He discusses the French Socialisme ou Barbarie group of Cornelius Castoriadis and Claude Lefort, noting their eventual abandonment of Marxism.

Time and space will allow only a few comments about these varying trends. Their main virtue, to me, should be clear: that *they use Marx's critique of political economy while rejecting statist interpretations.* From the beginning, *these trends focused on the autonomous self-activity of the working class and the oppressed*, as opposed to top-down, elite organizing. They examined the shop-floor activities of the workers, instead of focusing on the politics of parties and union bureaucracies. As their name indicates, the council communists of Germany and the Netherlands rejected the party-ruled state of Lenin in favor of rule by workers' and peasants' councils, while remaining revolutionary communists.

These far-left (sometimes called "ultra-left") trends had a variety of views about Marxist economic theory, often influenced by the period in which they developed. The views in this book have been particularly influenced by those of the council communist Paul Mattick, Sr. Castoriadis, on the other hand, came to reject Marxism altogether; he decided to call himself a "libertarian socialist," rather than an anarchist. Some of his reasons remain valid, I think, and are reflected in my criticisms of Marxism. Yet he was overly influenced by post-World War II prosperity. He decided that capitalist prosperity would go on indefinitely, thus disproving Marxist economics. His fellow-thinker, Maurice Brinton of the British Solidarity group, came to realize (in the 1980s) that these views "appear to have been proven wrong. There is most definitely an economic crisis of global proportions, the consequences of which include the driving down of [global] working class living standards" (2004, 217). In certain key ways, Marx's analysis had been shown to be accurate.

Nor is the thinking of all these trends radically democratic. Even when advocating workers' councils, they tended to advocate a centralized economy (as may be implied in the passage quoted from Mattick above). Worse, many were influenced by Amadeo Bordiga and those who followed him to completely reject workers' democracy. Some counterpoise "democracy" as a socialist goal to the "abolition of the law of value." But the law of value can be abolished only by replacing the exchange of commodities, the automatic market, and the capital/labor relationship by the conscious and collective decision making of freely associated producers. What is this but socialist democracy?

Even those far-left Marxists who stand for the autonomous self-management of the workers, still fail to analyze sufficiently how most of the Marxist movement developed into totalitarianism. What they lack is a critique of Marxism. Generally though, anarchists and far-left Marxists find many of the same issues contentious: Should revolutionaries form revolutionary organizations (not parties) to participate in broader movements? Should they join or support unions? National liberation struggles? United fronts?

Today many, perhaps most, radicals who regard themselves as anarchists do not accept a revolutionary proletarian strategy. They believe in gradually and peacefully building up counter-institutions and alternate lifestyles that is supposed to eventually replace the state and capitalism. This is essentially the old strategy of Proudhon, who, rejecting revolution, aimed to build a "mutual bank" to peacefully take over the French economy and replace the state.

It is disappointing to me that even many who identify with the autonomous (far-left) trend in Marxism similarly have come to reject proletarian revolution. Certainly not all, but many have replaced the working class with a concept of the "multitude" (Hardt and Negri 2000), or they water down the "proletariat" to include almost everyone, including peasants (Cleaver 2000). They deny that this is an epoch of capitalist decay and social revolution. They reject revolution (in the sense of popular insurrection democratically overturning the state) in favor of somehow withdrawing from capitalism, a strategy they call "exodus." They downplay workplace organizing in favor of somehow abolishing work in the foreseeable future.

Whatever the faults and limitations of Marx and Engels, Bakunin and Kropotkin, they were correct in advocating working class revolution. Despite their disagreements and their flaws, we stand on their shoulders. We build on their work. The international revolution of the workers and all oppressed is the only road to a classless, stateless, nonoppressive society, democratic and cooperative, of freely associated individuals, "in which the free development of each is the precondition for the free development of all" (Marx, *Communist Manifesto*, in Draper, 1998; 157).

Appendix to Chapter 8: Malatesta's Method for an Anarchist Economy

ONE of the most prominent attempts to present a model for a post-capitalist society is the theory of Parecon ("participatory economics"). One of its two founders, Michael Albert, wrote a book called *Parecon* in 2006 with the subtitle "Life Beyond Capitalism." Among other topics, he criticizes anarchists for lacking a vision of what institutions a new society would have. Anarchism, he says, "often dismisses the idea of vision, much less of providing a new political vision, as irrelevant or worse" (175). He makes the same charge against Marxists, even "libertarian Marxists or anarcho marxists" who are "the best Marxism has to offer" (159). In my opinion, there is truth in this accusation, especially regarding mainstream Marxists, but also libertarian Marxists and even anarchists. At the same time, it is exaggerated. His appreciation of the positive proposals of anarchists and other libertarian socialists is clouded by a desire to see fully worked-out programs for a new society, such as his Parecon, which leads him to ignore valuable, if less detailed, antiauthoritarian proposals.

For example, Albert quotes the great Italian anarchist Errico Malatesta's claim that anarchists want "the complete destruction of the domination and exploitation of person by person...a conscious and desired solidarity....We want bread, freedom, love, and science—for everybody." To which Albert replies, "Yes, yes, but how?" (176). This should not be a rhetorical question. How did Malatesta think everybody would achieve "bread, freedom, love, and science" in an anarchist society? While he did not have a developed blueprint, he did have an approach to developing anarchist institutions—the anarchist method.

Who Was Malatesta?

Born to a middle class Italian family in 1853, Errico Malatesta made his living as an electrician and mechanic. He personally knew Michael Bakunin and Peter Kropotkin, but unlike either, he lived to see the rise of fascism. He was imprisoned many times and sentenced to death three times. Due to political persecution in Italy, he spent over half his adult life in exile. He lived in the Middle East, in South America, in the United States, and, for about nineteen years, in Britain. Dying at seventy-nine in 1932, he had spent his last years under house arrest in fascist Italy.

As a young man, he participated in a couple of small, fruitless uprisings, attempts to spark peasant rebellions without first securing popular support (Pernicone 1993). He abandoned that for a more thought-out approach, but he never ceased being a revolutionary. He criticized those anarchist-syndicalists who believed that a revolution could be won nonviolently, simply by "folding arms" and calling a general strike. The capitalists and their state could not be beaten, he insisted, without some armed struggle to defend the workers. Because he was an advocate of popular revolution, however, he did not support the bomb-throwing and assassination tactics ("attentats") of anarchist terrorists (Malatesta 1999).

To Malatesta, "There are two factions among those who call themselves anarchists...supporters and opponents of organization" (1984, 84). These differences continue to this day. Malatesta was a pro-organizationalist anarchist. Aside from disagreements with anarchist-individualists, this was also his dispute with the anarchist-syndicalists. At the international anarchist conference of 1907, he debated the French anarchist Pierre Monatte (1881–1960). Monatte argued that anarchists should stop concentrating on small-group propaganda, putting out small newspapers and pamphlets, and should get into the work of building unions (syndicates) with other workers. Malatesta was not against building unions. In Argentina, he participated in building the Bakers' Union, one of the first labor unions there. But he opposed any tendency to dissolve anarchists into mass organizations. Effective unions had to include workers with all sorts of politics—revolutionary and reformist, statist and anarchist. Effective unions had to concentrate on winning reform struggles for better wages and conditions through bargaining with the capitalists—at least in nonrevolutionary times, which was most of the time. Therefore he insisted that revolutionary anarchists should also form specific organizations of anarchists only, to raise anarchist politics inside and outside of unions.

They were both right. Union work has helped anarchist militants greatly expand their influence among workers in several countries. At the same time, as became clear in

France, unions that the anarchist-syndicalists had worked to build became dominated by hardheaded "practical" officials. When World War I began, these union leaders became supporters of the imperialist war (which both Malatesta and Monatte opposed). Today, dual-organizationalist anarchists agree with Malatesta about the need for two types of organizations: the mass organizations (unions, community associations, etc.) and the narrower revolutionary organization with more political agreement. Even many of today's anarchist-syndicalists would agree.

The Anarchist Method

All his adult life, Malatesta identified with the tradition of libertarian (anarchist) communism. His goal was a society where all land and means of production were held in common and there was no use of money. Everyone would work as well as they could and would receive what they needed from the common store of products ("from each according to ability, to each according to need"). "Free associations and federations of producers and consumers" (1984, 17) would manage the economy "through an intelligent decentralization" (25). This would provide economic planning from below. His economic vision went along with the goals of abolition of the state, of national borders and nationalist passions, as well as with the "reconstruction of the family" (17) and the liberation of women.

However, over time he came to be critical of some anarchist-communist thinking as too simplistic. He criticized "the Kropotkinian conception...which I personally find too optimistic, too easy-going, too trusting in natural harmonies" (34). His was a more flexible communist anarchism. "Imposed communism would be the most detestable tyranny that the human mind could conceive. And free and voluntary communism is ironical if one has not the right and the possibility to live in a different regime, collectivist, mutualist, individualist—as one wishes, *always on condition that there is no oppression or exploitation of others*" (103; my emphasis).

Malatesta warned against believing that we have the Absolute Truth, as do religious people or Marxists. "One may, therefore, prefer communism, or individualism, or collectivism, or any other system, and work by example and propaganda for the achievement of one's personal preferences, but one must beware, at the risk of certain disaster, of supposing that one's system is the only, and infallible, one, good for all men, everywhere and for all times, and that its success must be assured at all costs, by means other than those which depend on persuasion, which spring from the evidence of facts" (27–28). His goal was free communism, but he understood that others preferred "collectivism," that is, an economy of common ownership that still rewards workers according to how much they work (Parecon includes a version of this); or an "individualism" that involved as much individual ownership and small-scale production as possible.

After a revolution, according to Malatesta

probably every possible form of possession and utilization of the means of production and all ways of distribution of produce will be tried out at the same time in one or many regions, and they will combine and be modified in various ways until experience will indicate which form, or forms, is or are, the most suitable. In the meantime, the need for not interrupting production and the impossibility of suspending consumption of the necessities of life will make it necessary to take decisions for the continuation of daily life at the same time as expropriation proceeds. One will have to do the best one can, and *so long as one prevents the constitution and consolidation of new privilege*, there will be time to find the best solutions. (104; my emphasis)

Is it likely that every region and national culture will choose the exact same version of libertarian socialist society? Will every industry, from the production of steel to the education of children be managed in precisely the same manner?

For my part, I do not believe there is "one solution" to the social problems, but a thousand different and changing solutions in the same way as social existence is different and varied in time and space. After all, every institution, project or utopia would be equally good to solve the problem of human contentedness, if everybody had the same needs, the same opinions, or lived under the same conditions. But since such unanimity of thought and identical conditions are impossible (as well as, in my opinion, undesirable) we must...always bear in mind that we are not...living in a world populated only by anarchists. For a long time to come, we shall be a relatively small minority.... We must find ways of living among nonanarchists, as anarchistically as possible. (151–152)

This would be true not only now but even after a revolution. We cannot assume that even when the workers have agreed to overthrow capitalism, they would agree to immediately create a fully anarchist-communist society. What if small farmers insist on being paid for their crops in money? They may give up this opinion once it is obvious that industry will provide them with goods, but first they must not be coerced into giving up their crops under conditions they reject.

After the revolution, that is, after the defeat of the existing powers and the overwhelming victory of the forces of insurrection, what then? It is then that gradualism really comes into operation. We shall have to study all the practical problems of life: production, exchange, the means of communication, relations between anarchist groupings and those living under some kind of authority.... And in every problem [anarchists] should prefer the solutions which not only are economically superior but which satisfy the need for justice and freedom and leave the way open for future improvements. (173)

It is precisely this flexibility, pluralism, and experimentalism that characterizes anarchism in Malatesta's view and makes it a superior approach to the problems of life after capitalism.

> Only anarchy points the way along which they can find, by trial and error, that solution which best satisfies the dictates of science as well as the needs and wishes of everybody. How will children be educated? We don't know. So what will happen? Parents, pedagogues and all who are concerned with the future of the young generation will come together, will discuss, will agree or divide according to the views they hold, and will put into practice the methods which they think are the best. And with practice that method which in fact is the best will in the end be adopted. And similarly with all problems which present themselves. (1974, 47)

Malatesta stopped calling himself a "communist," partly for the reasons given above. He also felt that the Leninists had effectively taken over the term (with the help of the capitalists, who agreed—insisted— that "communism" really was what the Bolsheviks claimed). "The communist-anarchists will gradually abandon the term 'communist'; it is growing in ambivalence and falling into disrepute as a result of Russian 'communist' despotism.... We may have to abandon the term 'communist' for fear that our ideal of free human solidarity will be confused with the avaricious despotism which has for some while triumphed in Russia" (1995, 20). If this was true in the 1920s, it is even more true by now, after about eighty years of Leninist/Stalinist rule under the banner of Communism, although the negative connotations of the term "communist" will vary from country to country. Malatesta eventually preferred the vaguer and more generic title of "socialist-anarchists." (1984, 143)

Related Views

Others have pointed to the flexible and experimental approach as central to the anarchist program. Bakunin, according to his friend James Guillaume, was a proponent of libertarian communism, but he did not believe it could be immediately and universally implemented. "In the meantime," Guillaume suggested, "each community will decide for itself during the transition period the method they deem best for the distribution of the products of associated labor" (1980, 362). This is very similar to Malatesta's approach.

In a more recent example, Paul Goodman, the most prominent US anarchist of the nineteen sixties, wrote:

> I am not proposing a system.... It is improbable that there could be a single appropriate style of organization or economy to fit all the functions of society, any more than there could be—or ought to be—a single mode of education, 'going to school,' that suits everybody.... In many functions [centralization] is economically inefficient, technologically unnecessary, and humanly damaging. Therefore we might adopt a political maxim: to decentralize where, how, and how much [as] is expedient. But where, how, and how

much are empirical questions. They require research and experiment." (1965, 27)

Unlike Malatesta, Goodman was a reformist, advocating a gradual approach to social change in the present society. Malatesta only advocated post-revolutionary "gradualism." Like Bakunin, Kropotkin, and Marx, Malatesta was a revolutionary. Similarly, Goodman advocated a "mixed system," (in the image he had of the Scandinavian countries), which included both capitalist corporations and cooperatives. Malatesta advocated a "mixed system" that explicitly excluded exploitation. It might include various forms of producer and consumer cooperatives and federations, as well as individual workshops or farms, but not capitalist enterprises that hired wage labor.

In certain respects, anarchist experimentalism resembles the Marxist concept of a post-revolution transitional period. According to his *Critique of the Gotha Program*, Marx expected society after a revolution to still suffer the lingering effects of capitalism. Society would gradually transform during this "first phase of communist society" so that, when production has increased sufficiently, it might achieve a "more advanced phase of communist society" (1974, 347). During this "transition," one might expect, a flexible and experimental attitude would be necessary.

Whatever the virtues of these ideas, they have been used by Marxists to justify Leninist-Stalinist totalitarianism— since, after all, we cannot expect post-revolutionary society to immediately fulfill the libertarian-democratic goals of classical communism. This was not Marx's intention, but it is how the "transitional period" concept has been used by Marxist-Leninists.

Neither Marx nor Malatesta believed it possible to immediately leap into a completely classless, moneyless, noncoercive, nonoppressive society. However, Marx's vision of the transition, despite its insights, tended to be more rigid than flexible; he laid out specific features of the lower phase of communism, which would come to pass in the course of the Historical Process. Malatesta preferred to make suggestions while leaving things open to pluralistic experiment. Marx also believed that some form of the state will be necessary—the "revolutionary dictatorship of the proletariat," —instead of thinking about how working people might protect and sustain their revolution without the bureaucratic-military machinery of a state. Malatesta advocated a popular militia.

To return to Michael Albert's challenge to Malatesta: "Yes, yes, but how?" Malatesta did not have a worked-out model for what anarchist socialism should be immediately after a revolution. He did not believe in such an approach. Yet he did not maintain that "anything goes." He advocated that working people take over the means of production and distribution and organize themselves to run them directly through free association and federation. It was just such a self-managed society that would be capable of an experimental and flexible method. However, this was "always on condition that there is no oppression or exploitation of others." He was not against speculation or programs, so long as they were presented with a certain modesty and willingness to see them change in practice.

He might have appreciated Albert's *Parecon* as a set of ideas for after a revolution, although not as a completed blueprint for what must be done. His goal was libertarian communism, but he was willing to see progress toward his goal go through various paths.

References for Further Reading

The following are suggestions for further reading. These are works I have on my shelves or refer to on-line and that appeal to me, even though I do not always agree with all the theories of the authors.

Introductory Readings

These introductory books are valued for being clearly written and covering the basic issues

Leontiev, A. (undated). *Political Economy: A Beginners' Course*. San Francisco: Proletarian Publishers. A "third period" Stalinist, with an exceptionally clear presentation of the basics of Marx's economic theory.

Cleaver, Harry (2000). *Reading* Capital *Politically*. San Francisco: AK Press/AntiTheses. A small book, by an "autonomous Marxist," which derives Marxist economics entirely from, Chapter 1 of *Capital*, Vol. I.

Fine, Ben, & Saad-Filho, Alfredo (2010). *Marx's "Capital"* (5th Ed.). London/ NY: Pluto Press.

Harvey, David (2010). *A Companion to Marx's* Capital. London/New York: Verso.

Disputed Topics in Marx's Economic Theory

The major area of controversy in the theory of Marx's critique of political economy revolves around the question of value: the labor theory of value, the "transformation prob-lem" (value into prices), the tendency of the rate of profit to fall, business cycles and their crashes. The single best book, which is up-to-date on current arguments, is the first book below.

Kliman, Andrew (2007). *Reclaiming Marx's "Capital": A Refu-tation of the Myth of Inconsistency.* Lanham, MD: Lex-ington Books/Rowman & Littlefield.

Mattick, Paul (1969). *Marx and Keynes: The Limits of the Mixed Economy.* Boston, MA: Extending Horizons/Por-ter Sargent. Other books by Paul Mattick, Sr., are well worth reading; he was a leading economist of the liber-tarian Marxist council communist trend.

Grossman, Henryk (1992). *The Law of Accumulation and Breakdown of the Capitalist System, Being also a The-ory of Crises* (J. Banaji, trans.). London: Pluto Press. Although an unconventional Stalinist, his brilliant eco-nomic theory greatly influenced the libertarian Mattick.

Crisis: The Great Recession and Since

Daum, Walter, and Matthew Richardson (2010). "Marx-ist Analysis of the Capitalist Crisis: Bankrupt System Drives Toward Depression." *Proletarian Revolution,* 82, 48, 35–45. http://lrp-cofi.org/pdf.html. Perhaps the sin-gle best statement.

Goldner, Loren (2008). "The Biggest 'October Surprise' of All: A World Capitalist Crash." http://home.earthlink.net/%7Elrgoldner/october.html.

Mattick, Paul, Jr. (2011*). Business As Usual: The Economic*

Crisis and the Failure of Capitalism. London: Reaktion Books.

Kliman, Andrew (2012). *The Failure of Capitalist Production: Underlying Causes of the Great Recession.* New York: Pluto Press.

Foster, John Bellamy, and Fred Magdoff (2009). *The Great Financial Crisis: Causes and Consequences.* New York: Monthly Review Press.

Bibliography

Albert, Michael (2006). *Realizing Hope: Life Beyond Capitalism*. London/New York: Zed Books.

Amin, Samir (2012). "The Center Will Not Hold." *Monthly Review*, 63/8, 45–57.

Anarchist Federation (2006). *Resistance to Nazism. Shattered Armies: How the Working Class Fought Nazism and Fascism*. London: Anarchist Federation Pamphlet.

Aronson, Ronald (1995). *After Marxism*. New York: Guilford Press.

ASP (1989). *Red Years, Black Years: Anarchist Resistance to Fascism in Italy* (from Rivista Anarchica). London: ASP.

Bakunin, Michael (1980). *Bakunin on Anarchism* (S. Dolgoff, ed.). Montréal: Black Rose Books.

Barrot, Jean [Gilles Dauvé], and Francois Martin (1974). *Eclipse and Re-emergence of the Communist Movement*. Detroit: Black and Red.

Bordiga, Amadeo (2003). *Proletarian Dictatorship and Class Party*. http://www.marxists.org/archive/bordiga/works/1951/class-party.htm.

Borsodi, Ralph (1933). *Flight from the City: An Experiment in Creative Living on the Land.* New York: Harper & Row.

Brinton, Maurice (2004). *For Workers' Power: The Selected Writings of Maurice Brinton* (David Goodway, ed.). Oakland: AK Press.

Buber, Martin (1958). *Paths in Utopia* (R.F.C. Hull, trans.). Boston: Beacon Press.

Cleaver, Harry (2000). *Reading* Capital *Politically.* San Francisco: AK Press/AntiTheses.

Daum, Walter (1990). *The Life and Death of Stalinism: A Resurrection of Marxist Theory.* New York: Socialist Voice.

Draper, Hal (1978). *Karl Marx's Theory of Revolution: Vol. II: The Politics of Social Classes.* New York: Monthly Review Press.

_____ (1986). *Karl Marx's Theory of Revolution*: Vol. III: *The "Dictatorship of the Proletariat."* New York/London: Monthly Review Press.

_____ (1987). *The "Dictatorship of the Proletariat" from Marx to Lenin.* New York: Monthly Review Press.

_____ (1998). *The Adventures of The Communist Manifesto.* Berkeley: Center for Socialist History.

Engels, Frederick (1954). *Anti-Dühring: Herr Eugen Dühring's Revolution in Science.* Moscow: Foreign Languages Publishing.

_____ (1972). *The Origin of the Family, Private Property, and the State.* New York: International Publishers.

_____ (1975). *The Housing Question.* Moscow: Progress Publishers.

Foster, John Bellamy (2000). *Marx's Ecology: Materialism and Nature.* New York: Monthly Review Press.

Geras, Norman (1976). *The Legacy of Rosa Luxemburg.* London: Verso.

Federici, Silvia (2004). *Caliban and the Witch: Women, the Body, and Primitive Accumulation.* Brooklyn NY: Autonomedia.

Goldner, Loren (1997). *Communism Is the Material Human Community: Amadeo Bordiga Today.* Baltimore: Collective Action Notes.

Goodman, Paul (1965). *People or Personnel: Decentralizing and the Mixed System.* New York: Random House.

Grossman, Henryk (1992). *The Law of Accumulation and Breakdown of the Capitalist System: Being Also a Theory of Crises* (J. Banaji, trans.). London: Pluto Press.

Guillaume, James (1980). "On Building the New Social Order." In Sam Dolgoff (ed.), *Bakunin on Anarchism* (pp. 356–379). Montréal: Black Rose Books.

Hardt, Michael, and Antonio Negri (2000). *Empire*. Cambirdge, MA: Harvard University Press.

Harvey, David (2010). *A Companion to Marx's* Capital. London/NY: Verso.

Hobson, Christopher Z., and Ronald D. Tabor (1988). *Trotskyism and the Dilemma of Socialism*. NY/Westport CT: Greenwood Press.

International Communist Current (1992). *The Italian Communist Left 1926–45: A Contribution to the History of the Revolutionary Movement*. London: I.C.C.

_____ (2001). *The Dutch and German Communist Left: A Contribution to the History of the Revolutionary Movement*. London: I.C.C.

Jackson, J. Hampden (1962). *Marx, Proudhon, and European socialism*. New York: Collier Books.

Kliman, (2012). *The Failure of Capitalist Production: Underlying Causes of the Great Recession*. London: Pluto Press.

Kropotkin, Peter (2002). *Anarchism: A Collection of*

Revolutionary Writings (R. Baldwin, ed.). Mineola, NY: Dover Publications.

Lappe, Frances Moore (October 2011). "The Food Movement: Its Power and Possibilities." *The Nation*, 293, 11–15.

Leier, Mark (2006). *Bakunin: The Creative Passion.* New York: Thomas Dunne Books/St. Martin's Press.

Malatesta, Errico (1974). *Anarchy.* London: Freedom Press.

_____ (1984*). Errico Malatesta: His Life and Ideas* (Vernon Richards, ed.). London: Freedom Press.

_____ (1995). *The Anarchist Revolution: Polemical Articles 1924–1931* (Vernon Richards ed.). London: Freedom Press.

_____ (1999). *Anarchism and Violence: Selections from Anarchist Writings 1896–1925.* Los Angeles: ICC.

Marx, Karl (1906*). Capital: A Critique of Political Economy,* Vol. I: *The Process of Capitalist Production* (F. Engels, ed.). New York: Modern Library.

_____ (1935). *The Poverty of Philosophy.* Moscow: Co-operative Publishing Society.

_____ (1967a). *Capital: A Critique of Political Economy,*

Vol. II: The Process of Circulation of Capital (F. Engels, ed.). NewYork: International Publishers.

_____ (1967b). *Capital: A Critique of Political Economy*, Vol. III: *The Process of Capitalist Production as a Whole* (F. Engels, ed.). New York: International Publishers.

_____ (1992). *The First International and After: Political Writings*, Vol. I (D. Fernbach, ed.). London: Penguin Books.

Marx, Karl, and Frederick Engels (1971). *On the Paris Commune.* Moscow: Progress Publishers.

_____ (1998). *The Communist Manifesto.* In H. Draper, *The Adventures of The Communist Manifesto*, 99–185.

Mattick, Paul (1969). *Marx and Keynes: The Limits of the Mixed Economy.* Boston: Extending Horizons/Porter Sargent.

Mattick, Paul (1978). *Anti-Bolshevik Communism.* Monmouth, Wales, UK: Merlin Press.

Mattick, Paul (1981). *Economic Crisis and Crisis Theory* (P. Mattick, Jr., trans.). London: Merlin Press.

Mattick, Paul (1983). *Marxism: Last Refuge of the Bourgeoisie?* (ed. Paul Mattick, Jr.). Armonk, NY: M.E. Sharpe.

McKay, Iain (2008). *An Anarchist FAQ,* Vol. I. Edinburgh, UK: AK Press.

McKay, Iain (2011). "Introduction." In Proudhon, J-P, *Property is Theft! A Pierre-Joseph Proudhon Anthology* (I. McKay, ed.). Oakland: AK Press.

McKay, Iain (2012). "Laying the Foundations: Proudhon's Contribution to Anarchist Economics." In D. Shannon, A. J. Nocella, II, & J. Asimakopoulos (eds.). *The Accumulation of Freedom: Writings on Anarchist Economics.* Oakland: AK Press.

Milstein, Cindy (2010). *Anarchism and Its Aspirations.* Oakland: AK Press/Institute for Anarchist Studies.

Pannekoek, Anton (2003). *Workers' Councils.* Oakland: AK Press.

Pernicone, Nunzio (1993). *Italian Anarchism, 1864–1892.* Princeton, NJ: Princeton University Press.

Price, Wayne (2007). *The Abolition of the State: Anarchist & Marxist Perspectives.* Bloomington, IN: Authorhouse.

Price, Wayne (2010). *Anarchism & Socialism: Reformism or Revolution?* Edmonton, Alberta Canada: thoughtcrime ink.

Rachleff, Peter J. (1976). *Marxism and Council*

Communism: The Foundation for Revolutionary Theory for Modern Society. New York: Revisionist Press.

Rivista Anarchia (1989). *Red Years, Black Years: Anarchist Resistance to Fascism in Italy* (Alan Hunter, trans.). London: ASP.

Schmidt, Michael, & van der Walt, Lucien (2009). *Black Flame: The Revolutionary Class Politics of Anarchism and Syndicalism.* Oakland: AK Press.

Sherover-Marcuse, Erica (1986). *Emancipation and Consciousness: Dogmatic and Dialectical Perspectives in the Early Marx.* Oxford UK: Basil Blackwell.

Tabor, Ron (August 2004). "The Dialectics of Ambiguity: The Marxist Theory of History." *The Utopian: A Journal of Anarchism and Libertarian Socialism.* Vol. 4. http://utopianmag.com/archives/the-dialectics-of-ambiguity.

Thomas, Paul (1980). *Karl Marx and the Anarchists.* London/Boston: Routledge & Kegan Paul.

Trotsky, Leon (1971). *The Struggle Against Fascism in Germany.* New York: Pathfinder Press.

van der Linden, Marcel (2009). *Western Marxism and the Soviet Union: A Survey of Critical Theories and Debates Since 1917* (J. Bendien, trans.). Chicago: Haymarket Books.

Vogel, Lise (1983). *Marxism and the Oppression of Women: Toward a Unitary Theory.* New Brunswick, NJ: Rutgers University Press.

Support AK Press!

AK Press is one of the world's largest and most productive anarchist publishing houses. We're entirely worker-run and democratically managed. We operate without a corporate structure—no boss, no managers, no bullshit. We publish close to twenty books every year, and distribute thousands of other titles published by other like-minded independent presses from around the globe.

The Friends of AK program is a way that you can directly contribute to the continued existence of AK Press, and ensure that we're able to keep publishing great books just like this one! Friends pay a minimum of $25 per month, for a minimum three month period, into our publishing account. In return, Friends automatically receive (for the duration of their membership), as they appear, one free copy of every new AK Press title. They're also entitled to a 20% discount on everything featured in the AK Press Distribution catalog and on the website, on any and every order. You or your organization can even sponsor an entire book if you should so choose!

There's great stuff in the works—so sign up now to become a Friend of AK Press, and let the presses roll!

Won't you be our friend? Email friendsofak@akpress.org for more info, or visit the Friends of AK Press website: http://www.akpress.org/programs/friendsofak